Maternity Clothes

Maternity Clothes

Simple patterns to make while you wait

Lynn Cardy & Alan Dart

Bell & Hyman

First published in 1982 by
BELL & HYMAN LIMITED
Denmark House
37-39 Queen Elizabeth Street
London SE1 2QB

British Library Cataloguing in Publication Data
Cardy, Lynn
Maternity clothes
1. Dressmaking – Patterns
I. Title   II. Dart, Alan
646.4'04   TT649

ISBN 0 7135 1313 6 Pbk

Designed by Colin Lewis
Typeset by Computerset Ltd, Oxford
Printed in Great Britain by The Pitman Press, Bath

Contents

Introduction

Waiting for the arrival of your bundle of joy can be the most exciting time of your life. It can also seem the longest nine months of it too, particularly if you can't afford to dress as you'd like, to make you feel confident and at ease. You can't avoid changing at least some part of your wardrobe, but why should you have to pay a fortune for clothes you may never wear again? A few simple but stylish garments you can make yourself are the ideal answer.

Maternity Clothes hopes to see you through those vital months and help you enjoy your pregnancy, feeling fine and looking smashing.

The first three months: Even though your actual measurements may alter very little, some women feel unwell and need clothes that are comfortable as well as smart. This is particularly vital if you are working right up to the last weeks in a demanding career.

The second three months: You start to 'look' pregnant and these are the months when you feel at your best. Your hair and complexion were never better and you generally look and feel great. This is also the time when you'll need some new and really attractive clothes to accommodate your 'bump'.

The last three months: You can feel a little like a beached whale, and that last month seems endless. Every social occasion brings nightmarish problems. You don't want to spend a fortune on special maternity clothes so near the end of your pregnancy. You do have a little time on your hands – but not the energy for trailing around the shops trying on clothes. Well, why not try a little gentle dressmaking? The patterns are really easy to draft and the clothes simple to knit and sew. It's also the perfect time to make all those accessories you might need for your hospital stay.

Enjoy your waiting time.

Before you start to sew

Each woman's body reacts in a totally different way when she becomes pregnant. Some are lucky enough to put on very little weight and need relatively few specialised clothes. Others seem to gain their 'bump' in the first few months and then keep on growing in all directions. Making your own maternity clothes is a wise move, enabling you to get a good personal fit.

Sizes
The patterns in the book refer to sizes 10, 12 and 14. This, of course, is your pre-pregnancy size and although the maternity clothes are bigger you must stick to your original size when cutting the patterns. As a guide, here is a list of basic sizes. Select your pre-pregnancy size and that will be the size you'll need to cut.

	10	12	14
Bust	87cm (34in)	92cm (36in)	102cm (38in)
Waist	67cm ($26\frac{1}{2}$in)	71cm (28in)	81cm (30in)
Hips	92cm (36in)	97cm (38in)	107cm (40in)

All the pattern pieces in the book are drawn to fit size 12. To alter them to your own size simply follow these steps.

For size 10: Draft the pattern and then trim 13mm ($\frac{1}{2}$in) from the *side* seams and *underarm* sleeve seams.

For size 12: Draft the pattern as it appears in the book.

For size 14: Draft the pattern adding 13mm ($\frac{1}{2}$in) to *side* seams and *underarm* sleeve seams.

The lines where you should make these alterations are marked with a broken line on the graph patterns in the book.

Cutting the pattern
The instructions in this book include, for each garment, a cutting guide for every pattern piece marked out in squares representing 5cm (2in). To prepare the actual pattern you will need some pattern guide paper ruled up into 5cm (2in) squares (manufacturer's details on page 128). Mark with a pencil on this special paper the exact position of all the points shown on the reduced-scale pattern in the book. Join up the points with curved or straight lines until you have a full-scale replica. Remember to include any extra instructions or fold lines.

Next, note the appropriate measurements on yourself for the type of garment you are making. For blouses, jackets and coats, check your back length and underarm seam. For trousers, shorts and dungarees, check your inside leg measurement and length from crutch to waist. Compare the size of the actual pattern piece with your own measurements and then enlarge or trim it where necessary.

Preparing to cut the fabric
With each set of instructions in the book, there is a small diagram showing the correct way to arrange the pattern pieces on your fabric. Using this as a guide, lay out the pattern pieces carefully and pin them. (Buy extra material if you are using a one-way fabric, such as velvet or corduroy, because all the pattern pieces must then run in one direction.) 1.5cm ($\frac{5}{8}$in) seam turnings are allowed for on all patterns, except where stated in the sewing instructions.

Before you start to knit

For good results use the yarns recommended. Yarns from different manufacturers vary quite considerably. If you have difficulty in obtaining them, write to the manufacturer named on page 128.

Before starting to knit your chosen pattern it is vital that you check your tension carefully. If it's not correct the garment will be the wrong size. To check tension, with the correct size needles, work the amount of stitches and rows required to make a 10cm (4in) square. Pin out and press lightly. If the square is larger than 10cm (4in) try a smaller needle size. If the square is smaller try a larger size needle.

When the garment pieces have been worked, pin the shapes out flat and press lightly. Check instructions on the ball band of your yarn, as some yarns can be pressed damp, some dry and some not at all. One important point – never press the ribbing.

Abbreviations

alt	Alternate
beg	Beginning
c6b	Cable 6 back – slip next 3 sts on to cable needle and leave at back of work, K3, then knit sts from cable needle.
c6f	Cable 6 front – slip next 3 sts on to cable needle and leave at front of work, K3, then knit sts from cable needle.
ch	Chain
cont	Continue
dc	Double crochet
dec	Decrease
g.st	Garter stitch – every row knit
inc	Increase
K	Knit
M1	Make 1 stitch
P	Purl
patt	Pattern
PSSO	Pass slipped stitch over
rem	Remaining
sl	Slip
st.st	Stocking stitch – one row K, one row P
st(s)	Stitch(es)
tog	Together
tbl	Through back of loop
tr	Treble
t.ch	Turning chain
yrn	Yarn round needle

DRESSES

1 Sailor smock dress

BASIC DRESS WITH CONTRAST YOKE

WITH RIBBON-TRIMMED SAILOR COLLAR ADDED

WITH BOUGHT LACE COLLAR AND LACE SEWN ROUND YOKE

The simplest of smock dresses, this one has a round neckline and will carry all manner of collars. Make it really dramatic by adding a huge, ribbon-trimmed sailor collar.

Dress

Fabric: 2.85m ($3\frac{1}{4}$yd) of 115cm (45in) wide fabric.
Notions: 45cm (18in) zip; 2 buttons for cuffs; optional ribbon trim.

1. Take the two back yoke sections, pin and sew darts. Press.
2. Take the two back dress sections and sew centre back seam up to the zip mark. Press open the seam up to the same mark.
3. Run a line of long gathering stitches along the top edge of one back section and gently draw up. Repeat on second dress back section.
4. With right sides together match bottom of yoke sections to gathered edges of dress sections and sew. Trim seam and press.
5. Turn back, press and tack the seam allowance down both centre back edges.

6. Pin and tack the zip 2.5cm (1in) down from the neck edge. Sew into place then remove tacking.
7. Take dress front section and run a line of gathering along top edge. Gently draw up until it measures the same as the bottom edge of the front yoke section. With right sides together pin gathered edge to yoke bottom and sew. Trim seam and press.
8. Then with right sides together, match the front and back section and sew shoulder and side seams. Press seams open and trim.
9. With right sides together, sew the two back facings to the front facing across shoulder seams. Press seams open.
10. Neaten all round outside curved edge. Turn over and press the seam allowance at the centre back edges of the facing. Tack down.
11. With right sides together and taking care to match shoulder seams, pin and sew facing to neckline of dress. Clip seams, trim right back. Turn facing to inside of dress and press the neckline well.

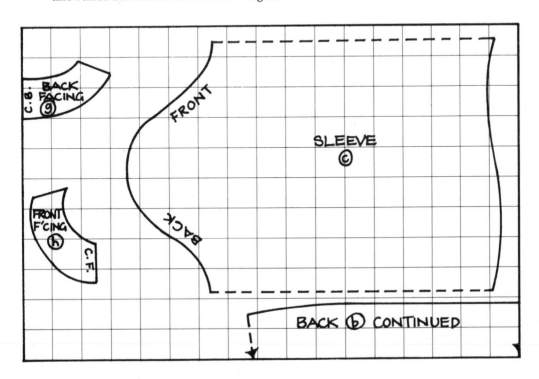

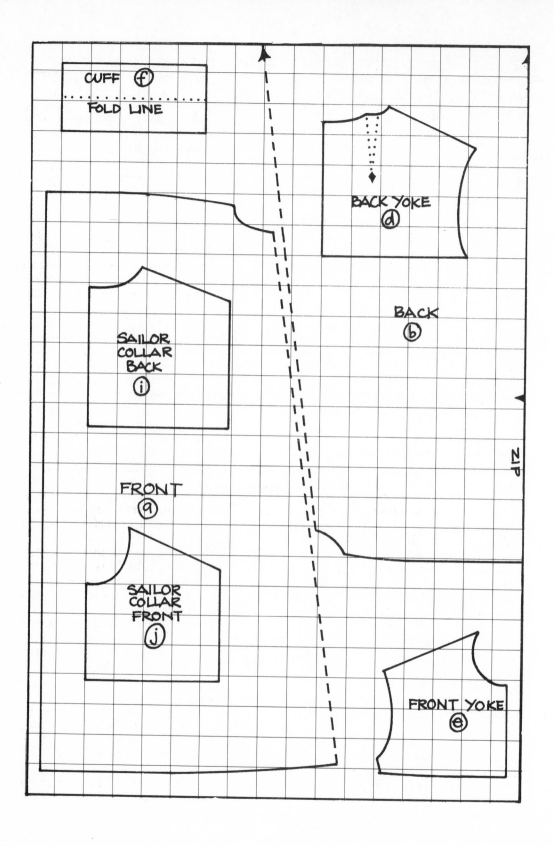

CUFF (f)

FOLD LINE

BACK YOKE (d)

BACK (b)

SAILOR COLLAR BACK (i)

FRONT (a)

SAILOR COLLAR FRONT (j)

ZIP

FRONT YOKE (e)

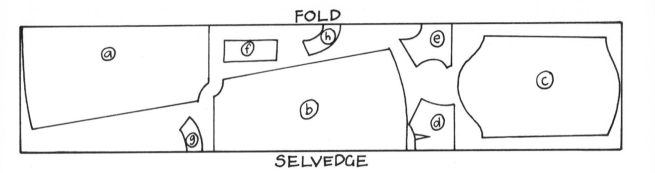

FOLD

SELVEDGE

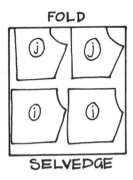

FOLD

SELVEDGE

12. Slipstitch the folded back edge of facing close to each side of the zip.
13. Take cuff section and with right sides together, fold along line indicated on pattern. Sew both short edges, trim seam – turn out and press. Repeat with second cuff.
14. Take sleeve section and with right sides together, sew underarm seam leaving 5cm (2in) unsewn. Press back the seam allowance at this opening and topstitch all round it. Repeat with second sleeve.
15. Run a line of gathering along bottom of sleeve and draw up, until it measures the same as the long edge of the cuff. Take one side of the free edge of the cuff and, with right sides together, pin and sew to bottom of sleeve. Trim seam and press towards cuff.
16. Turn under and press seam allowance on remaining free edge of cuff. Slipstitch into place using previous sewing line as a guide. Repeat with second sleeve. Topstitch all round cuff edge (see 'How To' Guide)

17. Mark and work one buttonhole on each cuff. Mark position of buttons and sew on.
18. Try on dress. Pin and sew the hem.

Collar
Fabric: 55cm ($\frac{5}{8}$yd) of 115cm (45in) wide fabric.

1. Take two back sections and one front section and, with right sides together, match and sew the two shoulder seams. Press open and trim.
2. Repeat with second set of front and back sections.
3. With right sides together match both collar sections and sew round outside edge. Leave neck edge unsewn. Clip corners, trim seams and turn out. Press well. Trim with lines of satin ribbon if desired.
4. Bind neck edge with wide bias binding, sewing it close to the edge of the collar. Press it to inside of collar. The extra binding will make the collar easier to attach to the dress.
5. To attach collar, slipstitch to inside of neck edge of dress. Do not machine collar on – slipstitching it will make it easier to remove for laundering.

Variations
a) This really is a most basic smock dress and has a simple round neck, ideal for trimming with lots of collars. You should find a selection in most big stores.
b) The sailor collar looks good on dresses of crisp striped cotton, or for colder days it looks marvellous against dark tartan fabrics.

13

2 Western-style dress

MADE IN CREAM LINEN WITH EMBROIDERED YOKE

MADE IN STRIPED FABRIC & WORN WITH PLAIN BANDANA

MADE IN CHECK FABRIC WITH FRINGE AT YOKE LINE

14

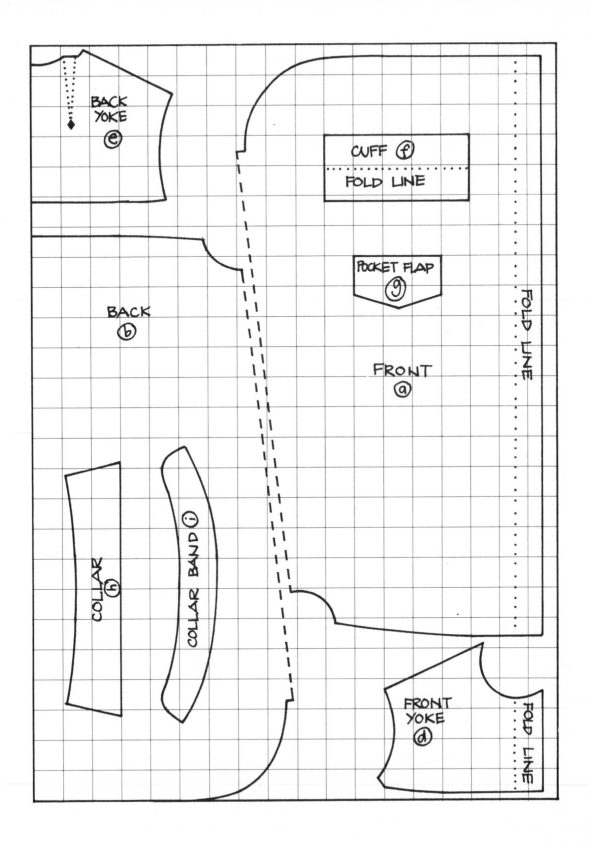

BACK YOKE (e)

CUFF (f)
FOLD LINE

POCKET FLAP (g)

BACK (b)

FRONT (a)

FOLD LINE

COLLAR (h)

COLLAR BAND (i)

FRONT YOKE (d)

FOLD LINE

15

Lots of authentic western details on this dress – embroidered yoke, tailored collar and decorative stud fastenings. It's very effective and much easier to make than it looks.

Fabric: 3.00m ($3\frac{3}{8}$yd) of 115cm (45in) wide fabric.

Notions: Coloured embroidery silks; 12 snap studs plus tool to apply them; stiffening for collar and band.

1. Mark and embroider roses on both front yoke sections, if desired (See 'How to' Guide for basic stitches.)
2. Take back yoke section and mark darts. Pin, sew and press them.
3. Take two pocket sections and, with right sides together, sew the two short sides and the sloping edges, leaving the top edge free. Trim seam allowance right back, turn through and press. Repeat with second pocket.
4. Take front section and, with right sides together, pin and stitch straight edge of pocket to bottom edge of front yoke – taking care to centre pocket onto yoke. Repeat with second pocket and yoke.
5. Take back section and run a line of gathering along the top edge. Draw up until it measures the same as the bottom edge of the back yoke section. With right sides together, pin back yoke to back dress section and sew. Press seam towards yoke.

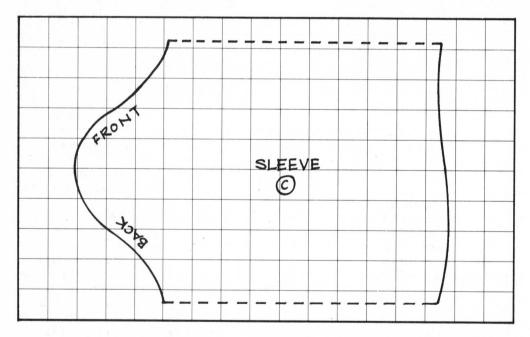

FOLD

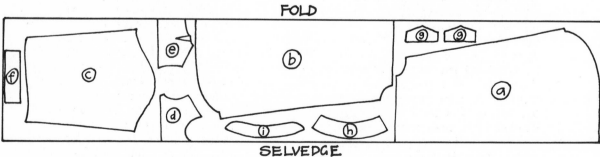

SELVEDGE

16

6. Take one front section and run a line of gathering along top edge. Draw up until it matches bottom edge of front yoke. With right sides together, pin and sew the pieces together. Press the seam allowance towards the yoke and the pocket towards the body of the dress. Repeat with the second front yoke and dress section.

7. Turn over and sew a tiny 6mm ($\frac{1}{4}$in) turning all down centre front edges of the dress fronts. Then fold over the front facing and press.

8. With right sides together match shoulder seams of front and back sections and sew. Press seam open.

9. Take the two collar sections and cut another single collar section from the stiffening.

10. With right sides together, match the fabric collar sections, place the stiffening collar on top and tack and sew through all thicknesses around the three outside edges, leaving the long neck edge free. Clip and trim the seam allowance and turn the collar out. Press.

11. Topstitch a line all round the outside edge of the collar, a sewing machine foot space away from the edge. (See 'How To' Guide.)

12. Next take the two collar bands and cut another single band in stiffening.

13. With right sides together, place one band on top of the other. Sandwich the collar between them, matching raw edges of collar with top edge of band. Take care to match centre back of the collar and centre back of collar band. Tack in place.

14. Take stiffening band and pin on top of one fabric collar band. Sew all round curved edge of collar band through all thicknesses, leaving long neck edge free. Trim seam allowance right back and clip curves. (See 'How To' Guide.) Turn out and press well.

15. With right sides together, match centre back of one free edge of collar to centre back of dress. Pin collar band all round neck of dress, taking care to match front edges of collar to front edges of dress. Sew.

16. Trim seam, clip curves and press the seam allowance towards the inside of the collar. Turn under and press the seam allowance on remaining free edge of collar. Slipstitch to inside of dress using previous line of stitching as a guide.

17. Take sleeve section and with right sides together, sew underarm seam, leaving 5cm (2in) unsewn at cuff end. Press back the seam allowance at this opening and topstitch all round it. Repeat with second sleeve.

18. Take cuff section and with right sides together, fold along line indicated on pattern. Sew both short edges, trim seams, turn out and press.

19. Run a line of gathering along bottom of sleeve and draw up, until it measures the same as the cuff. Take one side of the free edge of cuff and, with right sides together, pin and sew to bottom of sleeve. Trim seam and press towards inside of cuff.

20. Turn under and press the seam allowance on remaining free edge of cuff. Slipstitch into place using previous sewing line as a guide. Topstitch around outside edge of cuff. Repeat with second cuff.

21. With right sides together sew side seams of dress down to curved edge of hem. Press.

22. Pin in and sew both sleeves, taking care to match fronts and backs correctly. (See 'How To' Guide.)

23. Mark out the position of the press studs, evenly spaced. Mark one at the centre front of the collar band, two on the yoke, five down the front of the dress, one on each pocket flap and one on each cuff (use more if you like). Attach snap studs using the tool provided and following the manufacturer's instructions closely.

24. Try on dress and mark hem line. Trim away any excess. Turn over and sew a 6mm ($\frac{1}{4}$in) hem all round (including the opened out front facing).

25. Fold the front facings back onto the fronts of the dress (right sides together) and pin. Then stitch a line 1.5cm ($\frac{5}{8}$in) right round the hem of the

dress. Trim the corners of the facings, turn out and press. Then, using the line of stitching as a guide, fold up and press a hem, easing in any fullness as you go. Slipstitch into place.

Variations

a) For a really glamorous summer version of this dress, make it in cream linen embroidered with full-blown summer roses.

b) For winter how about a warm brushed cotton in muted checks, with a definitely western touch – some fringed braid, topstitched onto the front and back yoke?

c) In autumn, try making the dress without the collar, just a simple collar band. Then add a contrasting bandana (see our section on scarves).

3 Ethnic winter dress

YOKE KNITTED IN BRIGHT COTTON WITHOUT FAIR-ISLE, AND EMBROIDERED

DRESS MADE IN COTTON JERSEY

MAKE SLEEVES LONGER AND ELASTICATE CUFFS

SEW BRAID ROUND HEM

Cosy dress for winter – get inspired by the ethnic-look knitted collar and yoke with its tapestry effect. The rest of the dress is made in toning wool jersey.

This is a very simple dress to make, and for those with little knitting experience the yoke can of course be knitted plain.

Knitted yoke

Yarn: Of Double Knitting: 1 x 50g ball in four toning colours (A,B,C and D).
Needles: A pair of 3.5mm (No.9).
Tension: 21 sts and 27 rows to 10cm (4in) square, measured over st.st on 3.5mm (No.9) needles.
Measurements: To fit all sizes.

Back

With 3.5mm (No.9) needles and A cast on 55 sts and cont in st.st.
Work 2 rows.
Cont in pattern as follows:
Row 1: K1 B, *K5 A, K1 B *. Repeat from * to * to end.
Rows 2, 4 and 6: P, working colours as on previous row.
Row 3: K1 B, *K1 B, K3 A, K2 B *.
Row 5: K1 B, *K2 B, K1 A, K3 B *.
Rows 7 to 12: As rows 1 to 6, working A sts in B and B sts in C.
Rows 13 to 18: As rows 1 to 6, working A sts in C and B sts in D.
Rows 19 to 24: As rows 1 to 6, working A sts in D and B sts in A.
These 24 rows form the pattern.
Cont until 76 rows have been worked from cast on.
Shape shoulders: Keeping patt correct cast off 9 sts at beg of next 2 rows.
Cast off rem 37 sts.

Front

With 3.5mm (No.9) needles and A cast on 55 sts and cont in st.st.
Work 2 rows.
Cont in patt as given for back until 16 rows have been worked from cast on.
Divide for opening: Left side: Next row: Keeping patt correct work 28 sts, turn and slip rem 27 sts on to a stitch holder.
Dec 1 st at beg of next row (27 sts).
Cont in patt until 47 rows have been worked from cast on.

Shape neck: Next row: Keeping patt correct cast off 9 sts, patt to end.
Next row: Patt to end.
Dec 1 st at beg of next and every following alt row until 9 sts rem.

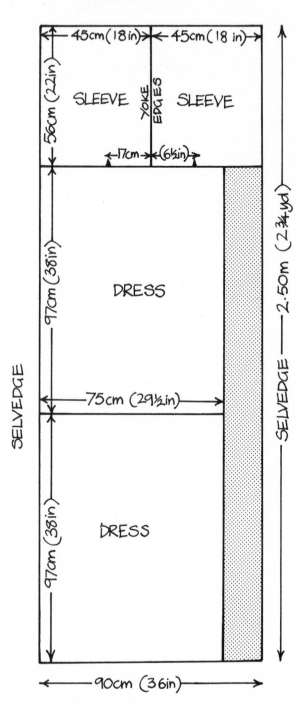

20

Cont without shaping until 76 rows have been worked from cast on.
Cast off.
Right side opening: Next row: Rejoin yarn to held 27 sts and keeping patt correct cont until 48 rows have been worked from cast on.
Shape neck: Next row: Keeping patt correct cast off 9 sts, patt to end.
Next row: Patt to end.
Dec 1 st at beg of next and every following alt row until 9 sts rem.
Cont without shaping until 77 rows have been worked from cast on.
Cast off.

Collar
Join shoulder seams. With 3.5mm (No.9) needles and A, and right side facing, pick up and K35 sts up right front neck, 37 sts across back, and 35 sts down left front neck (107 sts).
Work 22 rows g.st.
Cast off.

Dress
Sizes: One size fits sizes 10 to 14.
Fabric: 2.50m ($2\frac{3}{4}$yd) of 90 cm (36in) wide fabric.
Notions: Wool binding; one button.

1. Bind front opening of knitted yoke section with binding. (See 'How To' Guide.) Take a 9cm ($3\frac{1}{2}$in) length of binding and fold lengthways, stitch close to fold edge. Fold in half (raw edge to raw edge) and stitch to inside of right-hand neck edge to form button loop. (Adjust this to suit button size when stitching.)
2. Sew on button to left side of neck edge.

3. Take sleeve section and with right sides together, match, pin and sew yoke edge of sleeve to one side edge of knitted yoke. Press. Repeat with second sleeve.
4. Take one dress section and run a line of gathering along top edge. Draw up gathering gently, until it fits between the two marks indicated on the sleeve sections. With right sides together pin the dress section to the yoke/sleeve section between the two marks. Arrange the gathers neatly, so that most of the gathering is towards the centre (yoke section). Sew into place and press lightly. Repeat with second dress section.
5. With right sides together sew the underarm and side seam in one, taking care to match yoke seams at underarm. Trim this seam right back and neaten with zig-zag stitching or oversewing.
6. Turn up and sew a 6mm ($\frac{1}{4}$in) turning all round sleeve hem. Repeat on second sleeve, and around dress hem.
7. Try dress on and turn up hem of sleeves and dress hem as desired.

Variations
a) This dress has fore-arm length sleeves but by adding extra to the pattern pieces you could easily make long sleeves instead. Pretty them up by elasticating the sleeve hems.
b) For a real touch of luxury, knit the yoke in chenile yarn and make the main part of the dress in velour or crushed velvet.
c) Knit the yoke in plain bright cotton yarn and make the rest of the dress in softest cotton jersey – lovely for summer.

4 Wrap-round pinafore

MADE SHORT AS A SUNDRESS OR HOUSE APRON

WORN OVER FRILLED
WAIST SLIP AND
PIN TUCK BLOUSE

WORN OVER ELASTICATED SKIRT

22

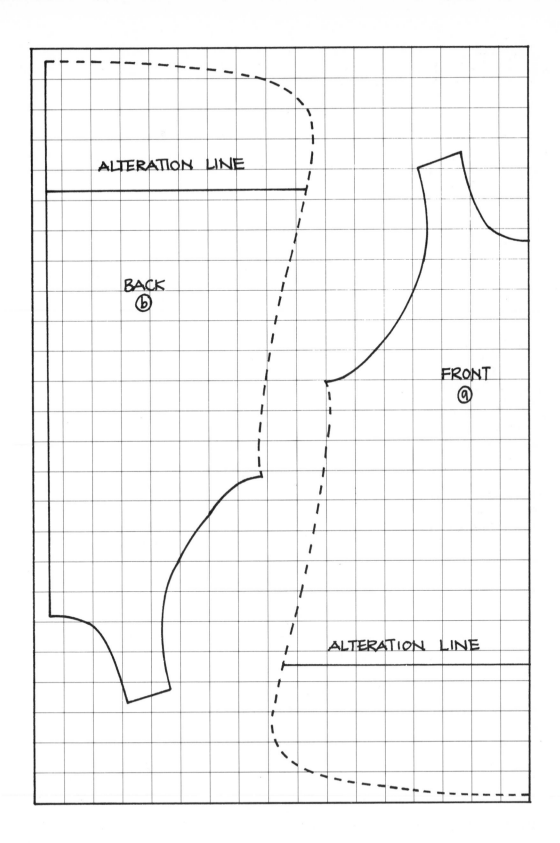

ALTERATION LINE

BACK
ⓑ

FRONT
ⓐ

ALTERATION LINE

A really super pinafore – for any season. Wear it over sweaters for autumn or winter, and over blouses for spring or summer. Make lots of them in mix-and-match colours and prints. Or really dress it up with ribbons and lace for a 'country' look.

Fabric: 1.60m ($1\frac{3}{4}$yd) of 115cm (45in) wide fabric.
Notions: 12m ($13\frac{1}{2}$yd) bias binding.

1. Take the two back sections and with right sides together, sew centre back seam. Press.
2. Next take front and back sections and with right sides together, sew shoulder seams. Press.
3. Starting and ending at the centre back, bind the neckline with the bias binding. (See 'How To' Guide.)
4. Starting and ending at the waist, bind all round the front curved skirt edge. Repeat on back section.
5. Starting and ending once again at waist level, this time bind all round armhole edge. Repeat on second armhole edge.

6. Take four 1m (1yd) lengths of bias binding, fold in half down the length of the binding and stitch through, close to the open edge.
7. Attach one of these ties at each of the four points where the armhole edge meets the side edges. Slipstitch to the underside very securely.
8. To wear, simply pop the pinafore over your head. Bring the back ties round to the front and tie in a bow at your waist under the front panel of the apron. Then take the front ties and tie them at the back, over the back panel. Couldn't be simpler!

Variations
a) Wear the pinafore over a brilliantly contrasting plain skirt (See pattern 19).
b) For a really feminine look, simply shorten the pinafore pattern and wear it over the pretty pin-tucked blouse (pattern 11) and the deeply flounced waist slip (pattern 27). The pinafore pattern has a simple alteration line to help you.
c) Worn alone it makes a cool and comfortable sundress for lazy days in the garden. Or a practical kitchen cover-up.

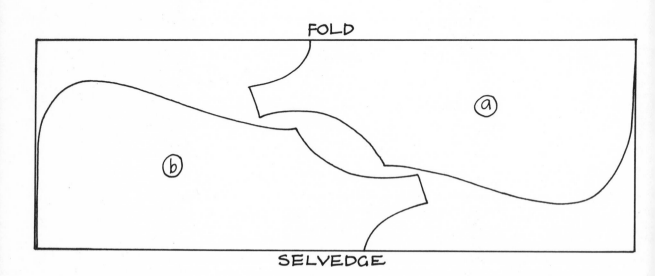

24

Two versions of the sailor smock dress (page 10).

5 Aran-style dress

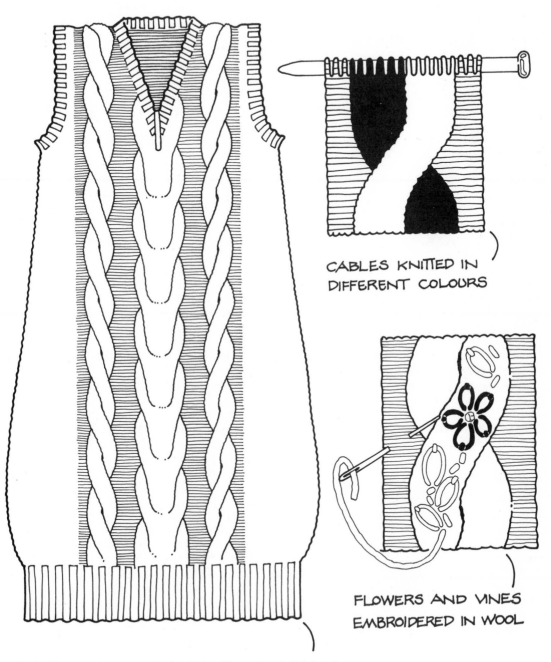

CABLES KNITTED IN DIFFERENT COLOURS

FLOWERS AND VINES EMBROIDERED IN WOOL

CHUNKY YARN WITH FRONT ARAN PANEL

Balloon dress and legwarmers (page 93).

Fast to knit, chunky cable dress which looks good over blouses and fine-knit sweaters. It's not the pattern for a beginner, but, if you have done some knitting before, do have a bash – it's really well worth it. Team it with coloured thick-knit tights.

Yarn: Of Chunky-style yarn: 16/16/17 50g balls.
Needles: A pair each of 5.5mm (No.5) and 6mm (No.4), and a cable needle.
Tension: 12 sts and 16 rows to 10cm (4in) square, measured over st.st on 6mm (No.4) needles.
Measurements: To fit sizes 10/12/14. Length: 109/112/115cm (43/44/45in).

Back
With 5.5mm (No.5) needles cast on 58/62/66 sts and work 8 rows K1, P1 rib.
Change to 6mm (No.4) needles and cont in st.st, comm with a K row.
Work 84/88/92 rows.
Dec 1 st at beg and end of next row.
Work 21 rows.
Repeat the last 22 rows once more (54/58/62 sts).
Shape armholes: Cast off 4 sts at beg of next 2 rows (46/50/54 sts).
Dec 1 st at beg of next and every following row until 38/42/46 sts rem.
Cont without shaping until 172/176/180 rows have been worked from cast on.
Shape shoulders: Cast off 9/11/13 sts at beg of next 2 rows.
Cast off rem 20 sts.

Front
With 5.5mm (No.5) needles cast on 58/62/66 sts and work 8 rows K1, P1 rib.
Change to 6mm (No.4) needles and cont as follows:
Next row: K 11/13/15, P2, (K1, inc 1 by knitting into front then back of next st) twice, P8, (K1, inc 1) four times, P8, (K1, inc 1) twice, P2, K11/13/15 (66/70/74 sts).
Next and every following alt row: P11/13/15, K2, P6, K8, P12, K8, P6, K2, P11/13/15.
Rows 1, 3 and 5: K 11/13/15, P2, K6, P8, K12, P8, K6, P2, K11/13/15.
Row 7: K11/13/15, P2, c6b, P8, c6b, c6f, P8, c6f, P2, K11/13/15.
Row 8: P11/13/15, K2, P6, K8, P12, K8, P6, K2, P11/13/15.
These 8 rows form the pattern.
Cont until 92/96/100 rows have been worked from cast on.
Dec 1 st at beg and end of next row.
Work 21 rows.
Repeat the last 22 rows once more (62/66/70 sts).
Shape armholes: Cast off 4 sts at beg of next 2 rows (54/58/62 sts).
Divide for neck: Left side: Next row: K2 tog, K3/5/7, P2, c6b, P8, K6, slip rem sts on to a stitch holder.
Next row: K the P sts and P the K sts of previous row.
Next row: K2 tog, K2/4/6, P2, K6, P8, K6.
Next row: P2 tog, P4, K8, P6, K2, P3/5/7.
Next row: K2 tog, K1/3/5, P2, K6, P8, K5.
Next row: K the P sts and P the K sts of previous row.
Next row: K2 tog, K0/2/4, P2, K6, P8, K3, K2 tog.
Cont twisting cable on row 7 and decreasing 1 st at neck edge every 3rd row until 11/13/15 sts rem.
Cont without shaping until 172/176/180 rows have been worked from cast on.
Cast off.
Right side: Next row: Rejoin yarn to held sts and K6, P8, c6f, P2, K5/7/9.
Next row: P2 tog, P3/5/7, K2, P6, K8, P6.
Next row: K2 tog, K4, P8, K6, P2, K4/6/8.
Next row: P2 tog, P2/4/6, K2, P6, K8, P5.
Next row: K5, P8, K6, P2, K3/5/7.
Next row: P2 tog, P1/3/5, P6, K8, P3, P2 tog.
Next row: K4, P8, K6, P2, K2/4/6.
Next row: P2 tog, P0/2/4, K2, P6, K8, P4.
Cont twisting cable on row 7 and decreasing 1 st at neck edge every 3rd row until 11/13/15 sts rem.
Cont without shaping until 173/177/181 rows have been worked from cast on.
Cast off.
Neckband (all sizes)
Join right shoulder seam. With 5.5mm (No.5) needles and right side facing pick up and K31 sts down left front neck, pick up loop between sts at centre front and K into back of it, mark this st with a coloured thread, pick up and K31 sts up right front

neck, and 20 sts across back (83 sts).
Next row: Work in K1, P1 rib to 2 sts before
marker, P2 tog, K1, P2 tog tbl, rib to end.
Next row: Work in rib to 2 sts before
marker, K2 tog tbl, P1, K2 tog, rib to end.
Repeat these 2 rows two more times.
Cast off in rib, still dec at front.

Armhole borders
Join left shoulder seam and neckband.
With 5.5mm (No.5) needles and right side
facing pick up and K54/58/62 sts round
armhole.
Work 6 rows K1, P1 rib.
Cast off in rib.

To make up
Press work according to instructions on
ball band. Join side seams. Press seams.

Variations
a) If you are a really experienced knitter,
try working the cables in a contrasting
colour.
b) Embroidery enthusiasts can really
show off their talents by embroidering
flowers and vines twisting up the cables.

6 Pinafore dress

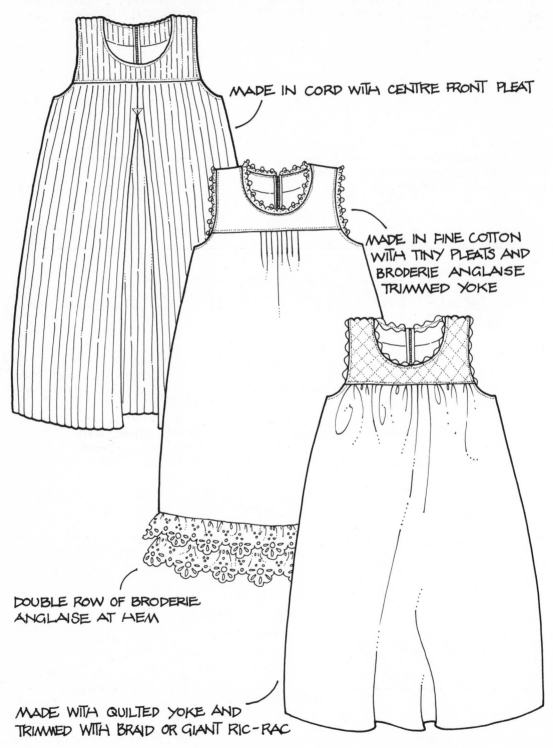

MADE IN CORD WITH CENTRE FRONT PLEAT

MADE IN FINE COTTON WITH TINY PLEATS AND BRODERIE ANGLAISE TRIMMED YOKE

DOUBLE ROW OF BRODERIE ANGLAISE AT HEM

MADE WITH QUILTED YOKE AND TRIMMED WITH BRAID OR GIANT RIC-RAC

A most versatile dress – you can create so many different looks with this one simple pattern. Take your pick from a deep inverted pleat to gathers or even pin-tucks. There simply has to be one that's just right for you.

Fabric: 2.40m ($2\frac{5}{8}$yd) of 115cm (45in) wide fabric.
Notions: 45cm (18in) zip; tiny hook and eye.

1. Take dress front section and fold in half lengthways with right sides together.
2. Stitch pleat down line indicated on pattern. Open out dress front and press pleat top.
3. Take dress yoke and with right sides together stitch bottom of yoke to top edge of dress front.
4. Take the two back sections and with right sides together stitch up to zip mark. Press seam and press back and tack seam allowance at zip opening.
5. Pin and tack zip into place 2.5cm (1in) down from neck edge. Sew zip into place.
6. Take the front and back sections and with right sides together sew side seams. Press seams open.
7. Take the front and back facing sections and with right sides together sew the side seams. Press the seams

open. Neaten the curving bottom edge of the facing with a zig-zag or oversewing stitches.
8. At the shoulder edges of both front and back facings turn over, press and tack back the seam allowances.
9. With right sides together, pin facing to dress top and sew as follows. Sew across back neck up to folded seam allowance on shoulder edge of facing. Repeat on other back neck section.
10. Sew from folded shoulder seam allowance right round armhole to second folded shoulder seam allowance. Repeat with second armhole.
11. Sew round front neck line from one folded shoulder seam allowance to the other. Trim and clip all seam allowances. Turn out front and back facings and press neck line and armhole edges.
12. With right sides together sew front and back dress sections together at shoulders. Press seam open, tuck seam allowance under folded edge of facing and then slipstitch the open shoulder seams of the facings together.
13. Fold back seam allowance at centre back of facing and slipstitch down close to zip.
14. Turn up and stitch hem as desired.
15. Catchstitch facing to side seam on inside of dress, to prevent it from riding up.

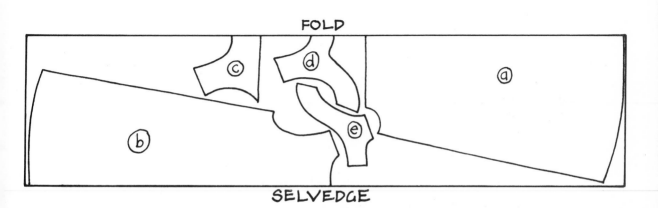

29

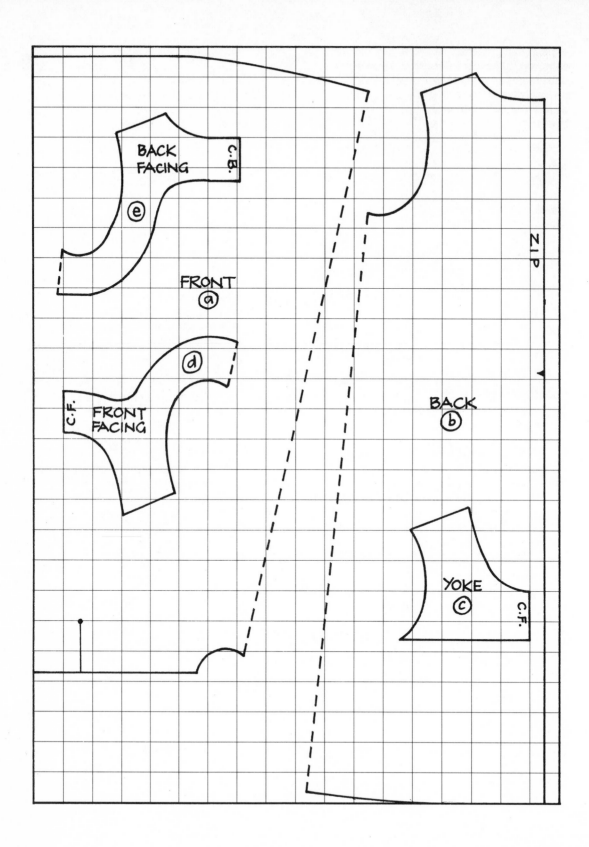

BACK FACING (e)

C.B.

FRONT (a)

FRONT FACING (d)

C.F.

BACK (b)

ZIP

YOKE (c)

C.F.

Variations

a) For winter, make the pleat-front dress in needlecord to wear over a ribbed woolly sweater (see pattern 10).

b) For autumn, make the dress in brushed cotton with a quilted yoke.

c) You needn't always make a pleat – for a different effect you can gather the skirt onto the yoke.

d) For a cool summer dress make the pinafore in fine white cotton. This time pin-tuck the skirt onto the yoke and trim the skirt with ready-flounced broderie anglaise.

7 Short party dress

HEADBAND TIED IN BOW

HEADBAND USED AS SASH
AFTER BABY

BRODERIE ANGLAISE

32

One dress you really will be able to wear after baby is born. Full and swirly, it can see you happily through any party. Wear the sash tied around your hair, peasant-style, while you're pregnant. And afterwards ... well, you can tie the sash tightly around your waist and we guarantee it won't look like a maternity smock.

Fabric: 3.80m ($4\frac{1}{4}$yd) of 115cm (45in) wide fabric.
Notions: 2.50m ($2\frac{3}{4}$yd) of 6mm ($\frac{1}{4}$in) elastic.

1. Take the two back sections and with right sides together, sew back seam. Press.
2. Take one sleeve section and with right sides together, match points A and B on dress front to points A and B on sleeve front. Sew between these two points, neaten and press. Repeat with second sleeve and dress front.
3. Repeat between points C and D on sleeves and dress backs.
4. With right sides together pin and sew side seams, starting at sleeve hem and ending at dress hem, taking care to match seams at underarms. Press and neaten.
5. Turn over and stitch a 6mm ($\frac{1}{4}$in) turning all round neckline and sleeve hems. Then turn over a further 13mm ($\frac{1}{2}$in) turning at neck and sleeve hems, leaving a small gap through which to insert elastic.
6. Slot elastic through neckline. Draw up

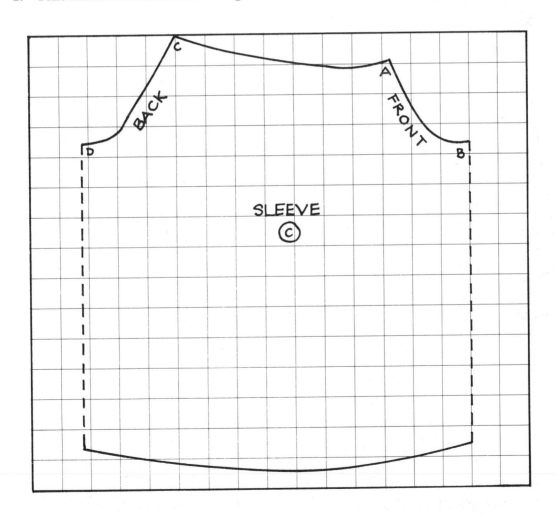

33

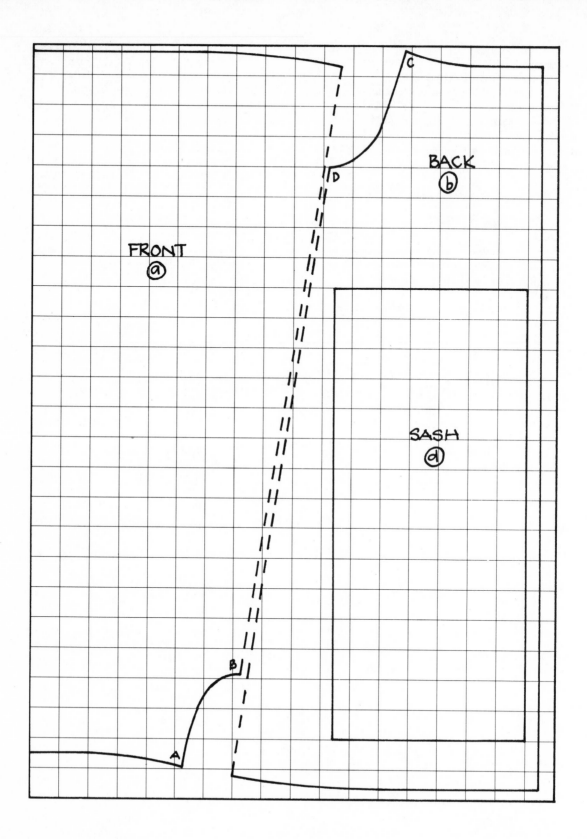

FRONT
(a)

BACK
(b)

C

D

SASH
(d)

B

A

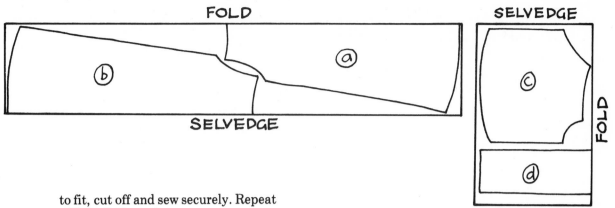

FOLD

SELVEDGE

ⓑ   ⓐ

SELVEDGE   ⓒ   FOLD

ⓓ

SELVEDGE

to fit, cut off and sew securely. Repeat with both sleeve hems.

7. Turn up and stitch hem to desired length.

8. Take sash, and with right sides together fold in half lengthways. Stitch along the long and one short edge, turn out and press. Slipstitch second short edge closed.

Variations

a) The basic dress trimmed with broderie anglaise and the sash worn as a scarf makes a stunning party dress while you're pregnant.

b) This will be one dress you'll be glad to wear after baby is born – tie the sash tightly round your newly returned waistline.

c) Make the dress in fine brushed cotton for a winter nightie. Run an extra line of shirring around the top of the sleeve for a real pre-Raphaelite look. The sash can keep your hair tidy.

8 Long evening dress and jacket

LONG DRESS BOUND WITH SATIN

SHORT DRESS AND JACKET WITH LACE COLLAR & CUFFS

LACE JACKET WITH SATIN YOKE AND BINDING ~ SLEEVES LEFT BELL SHAPED

Formal dress and jacket for truly grand occasions. The dress is starkly simple yet elegant, the jacket is soft and pretty. Accentuate this contrast by making the dress in something darkly dramatic like black velvet and team it with a jacket made from the softest lurex brocade, or deeply scalloped lace.

Fabric: *Dress:* 3.60m (4yd) of 115cm (45in) wide fabric. *Jacket:* 2.30m ($2\frac{5}{8}$yd) of 90cm (36in) wide fabric.

Notions: 50cm (20in) zip; 2.50m ($2\frac{3}{4}$yd) of satin binding; 70cm ($\frac{3}{4}$yd) of 6cm ($2\frac{1}{2}$in) wide lace (to match jacket fabric, straight on one edge and scalloped on the other); 2.00m of 1cm ($\frac{1}{2}$in) wide satin ribbon; 1.00m ($1\frac{1}{8}$yd) of narrow lace to trim jacket sleeves; tiny hook and eye.

Dress

1. Take two back skirt sections and with right sides together, sew up to the mark for zip. Press seam open.
2. Take one back yoke section and with right sides together, pin and sew bottom edge of back yoke to top edge of back skirt. Press seam open. Repeat with second back yoke and back skirt section.
3. Press back and tack the seam allowance at the centre back opening.
4. Pin and tack the zip into place. Sew, take out tacking and press lightly.
5. Take the two front skirt sections and with right sides together, sew front seam. Press open.
6. Take front yoke section and with right sides together pin yoke to skirt and sew. Press seam open.
7. With right sides together take front and back sections and sew shoulder seams. Press open.
8. Also with right sides together, sew side seams. Press open.
9. Starting and ending at centre **back** edges, bind all round neckline. (See 'How To' Guide.)
10. Starting and ending at underarm seam bind all round armhole edge. Repeat with second armhole.
11. Sew tiny hook and eye at centre back neck edge.

12. Try on dress and turn up hem as desired, slipstitch and press.

Jacket

1. Take jacket back section and run a line of gathering along the top edge. Draw up until it measures the same as the bottom edge of the yoke section.
2. With right sides together, pin yoke to back section and sew. Press.
3. Take one front jacket section and turn over and tack a 6mm ($\frac{1}{4}$in) turning down centre front edge. Then turn over a further 1.5cm ($\frac{5}{8}$in) hem and stitch down. Press. Repeat this on second front section.
4. Run a line of gathering along the top edge of one jacket front section and draw up until it fits front edge of the yoke.
5. With right sides together pin yoke to jacket front and stitch. Press. Repeat these last two stages on second front.
6. Take sleeve section and with right sides together, sew underarm seam and press. Repeat with second sleeve.
7. Turn up a 6mm ($\frac{1}{4}$in) hem around bottom of sleeve and stitch, then turn up a further 1.5cm ($\frac{5}{8}$in) and stitch. Slipstitch narrow lace to underside of sleeve hem. Repeat on second sleeve.
8. Run two lines of shirring around sleeve 5cm (2in) up from sleeve hem to form flounced cuff (see 'How To' Guide). Repeat on second sleeve.
9. Pin in and sew both sleeves. (See 'How To' Guide.)
10. Take the length of wide lace and stitch a tiny hem at both short edges. Run a line of gathering along straight edge and draw up to fit neckline.
11. With wrong sides together, pin and stitch lace to neck edge of jacket, carefully matching edge of lace with front edges of jacket. Seam allowance should be on right side of jacket.
12. Trim this seam right back to 6mm ($\frac{1}{4}$in) and press open.
13. Take the satin ribbon and find the half-way mark. Match this mark to the centre back of the jacket neckline.
14. Pin the ribbon around the neckline, covering the trimmed seam. Stitch

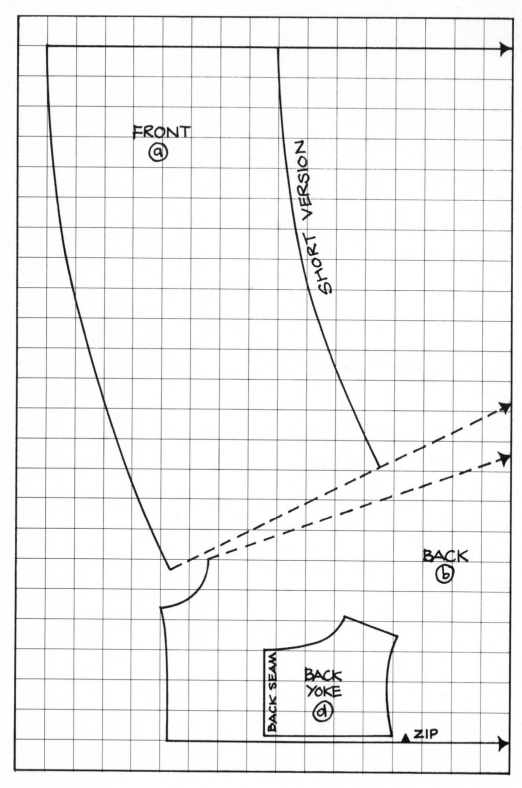

FRONT
ⓐ

SHORT VERSION

BACK
ⓑ

BACK SEAM

BACK YOKE
ⓓ

ZIP

Dress

38

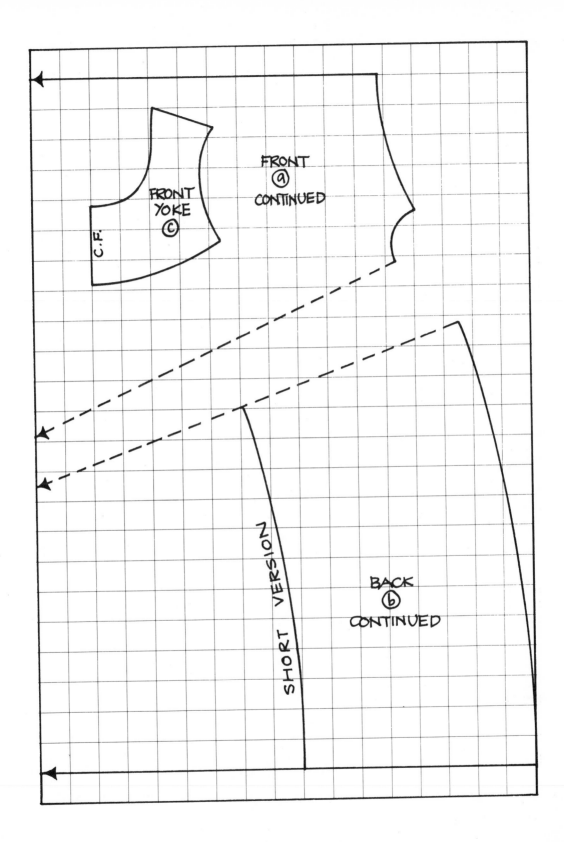

FRONT
(a)
CONTINUED

FRONT
YOKE
(c)

C.F.

SHORT VERSION

BACK
(b)
CONTINUED

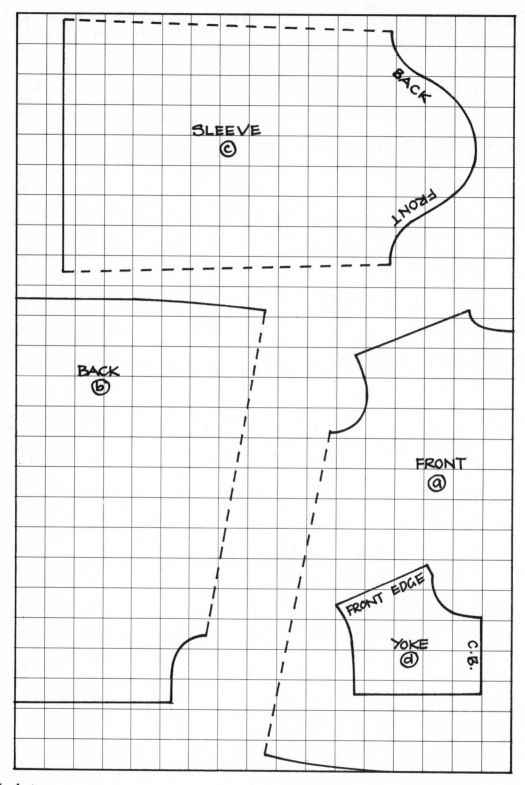

Jacket

the ribbon down with two lines of stitching close to the ribbon edges. The excess ribbon at the centre front edges forms the ties.

15. Turn up the jacket hem as desired and slipstitch.

Variations

a) Make this very simple evening dress in something really heavy like double crêpe to give it an almost sculptured look.

b) To contrast with the dress, make the soft jacket in a shimmery fabric shot with metallic glints.

c) For a real touch of luxury make the jacket in gorgeous scallop-edged lace, with a touch of satin at the yoke and simple bound neck and ties. For this style, make the most of the fabric and leave the sleeves bell-shaped.

d) You could also make it short for another very useful day dress.

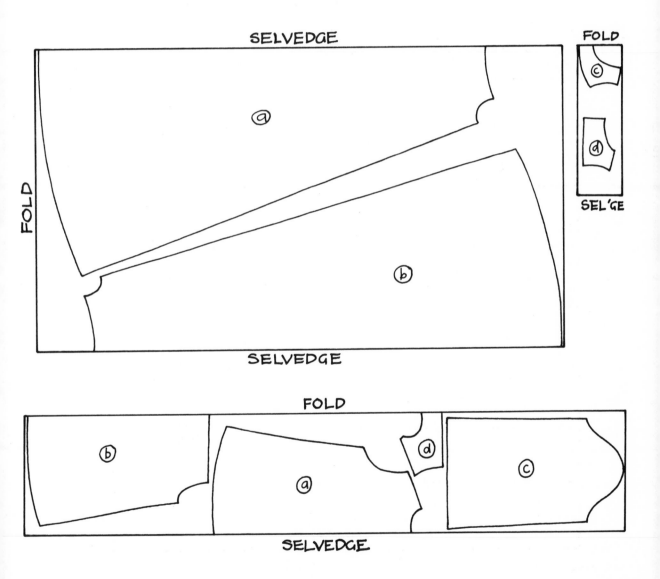

41

TOPS

9 Chunky picture sweater

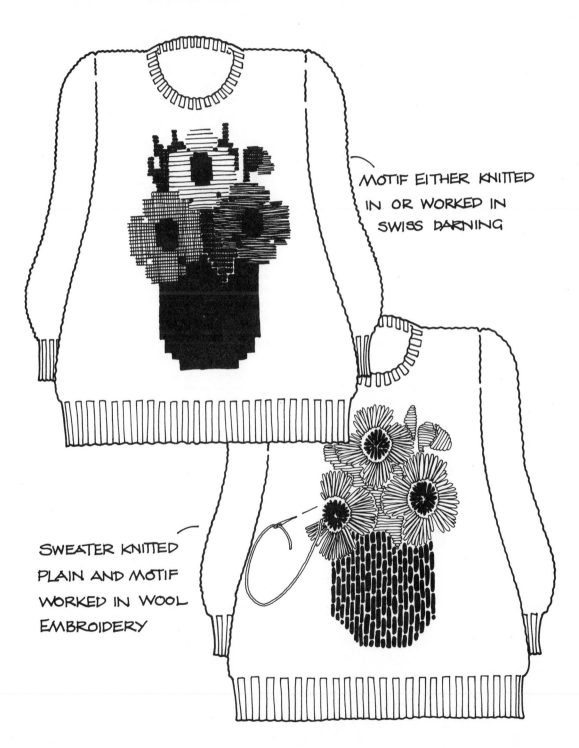

MOTIF EITHER KNITTED IN OR WORKED IN SWISS DARNING

SWEATER KNITTED PLAIN AND MOTIF WORKED IN WOOL EMBROIDERY

When it's not a secret any more and you just can't hide that bump, you might as well make a feature of it! Try this bright and jolly picture sweater – the wool is very chunky and we promise it won't take long to make. For timid knitters, make it plain but most definitely in a bright, bold colour.

Yarn: Of Chunky style yarn: 14/14/15 x 50g balls in main colour (MC) and 1/1/1 ball each of six contrasting colours.
Needles: A pair each of 5.5mm (No.5) and 6mm (No.4).
Tension: 12 sts and 16 rows to 10cm (4in) square, measured over st.st on 6mm (No.4) needles.
Measurements: To fit sizes 10/12/14.
Length: 61/64/67cm (24/25/26in). *Sleeve seam:* 45/46/47cm ($17\frac{1}{2}$/18/$18\frac{1}{2}$in).

Back
With 5.5mm (No.5) needles and MC cast on 59/63/67 sts and work 12 rows K1, P1 rib.
Change to 6mm (No.4) needles and cont in st.st comm with a K row.
Work 12/16/20 rows.
Dec 1 st at beg and end of next row.
Work 17 rows.
Repeat the last 18 rows once more (55/59/63 sts).
Shape armholes: Cast off 4 sts at beg of next 2 rows (47/51/55 sts).
Dec 1 st at beg of next and every following row until 41/43/45 sts rem *.
Shape shoulders: Cast off 10/11/12 sts at beg of next 2 rows.
Cast off rem 21 sts.
Front
With 5.5mm (No.5) needles and MC cast on 59/63/67 sts and work 12 rows K1, P1 rib.
Change to 6mm (No.4) needles and cont in st.st comm with a K row.
Work 8/12/16 rows.
Work motif: Next row: K13/15/17, K first row of graph reading from right to left, K to end.
Next row: P14/16/18, P second row of graph reading from left to right, P to end.
Cont in this manner, using separate balls of yarn for each colour change and twisting

where yarns meet, and follow shaping instructions as given for back to *.
Cont without shaping until 80/84/88 rows have been worked from cast on, ending with a P row.
Divide for neck: Left side: Next row: K15/16/17, turn and slip rem sts on to a stitch holder.
Dec 1 st at beg of next and every following alt row until 10/11/12 sts rem.
Cont without shaping until 96/100/104 rows have been worked from cast on.
Cast off.
Right side: Rejoin yarn to held sts, cast off centre 11 sts, K rem 15/16/17 sts.
Next row: P.
Dec 1 st at beg of next and every following alt row until 10/11/12 sts rem.
Cont without shaping until 97/101/105 rows have been worked from cast on.
Cast off.
Sleeves (2 alike)
With 5.5mm (No.5) needles and MC cast on 31/31/31 sts and work 12 rows K1, P1 rib.
Change to 6mm (No.4) needles and cont in st.st comm with a K row.
Work 2/4/6 rows.
Inc 1 st at beg and end of next and every following 7th row until there are 45/45/45 sts on the needle.
Cont without shaping until 70/72/74 rows have been worked from cast on.
Shape sleeve head: Cast off 4 sts at beg of next 2 rows (37 sts).
Dec 1 st at beg of next 2 rows.
Work 2 rows.
Dec 1 st at beg of next and every following row until 15 sts rem.
Cast off.
Neckband (all sizes)
Join right shoulder seam. With 5.5mm (No.5) needles, MC, and right side facing pick up and K15 sts down left front neck, 11 sts across centre, 15 sts up right front neck, and 22 sts across back (63 sts).
Work 6 rows K1, P1 rib.
Cast off in rib.
To make up
Press work according to instructions on ball band. Join left shoulder seam and neckband. Sew in sleeves. Join side and sleeve seams. Press seams.

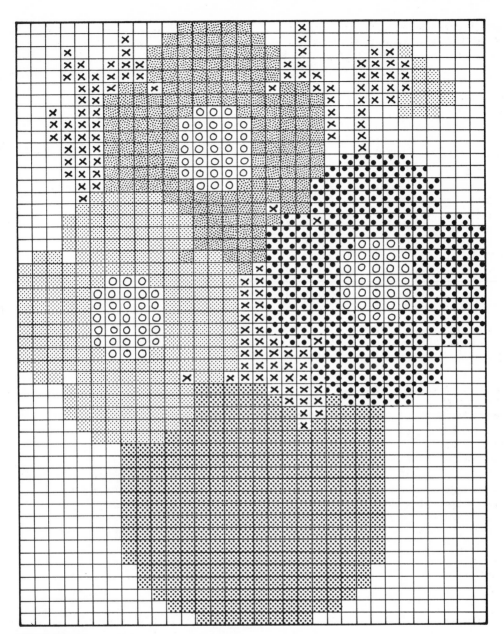

Variations

a) If you are hopeless at knitting motifs but would still like that pretty bunch of flowers, try Swiss Darning – it's so easy. (See 'How To' Guide.)

b) Knit in big brash stripes of clashing colour for casual weekend wear. Team it with our laced-front jeans (pattern 15).

Who says pregnant ladies have to look dull?

10 Ribbed polo-neck sweater

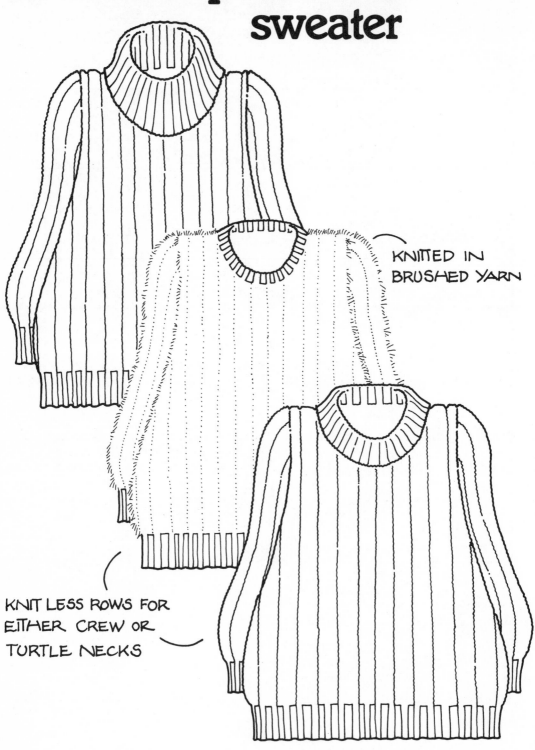

KNITTED IN BRUSHED YARN

KNIT LESS ROWS FOR EITHER CREW OR TURTLE NECKS

Make several of these useful sweaters in colours to match or tone with the rest of your maternity wardrobe. This sweater is specially designed to fit your 'bump' and it shouldn't ride up or wrinkle.

Yarn: Of Chunky-style yarn: 12/12/13 x 50g balls.
Needles: A pair each of 5.5mm (No.5) and 6mm (No.4).
Tension: 12 sts and 16 rows to 10cm (4in) square, measured over st.st on 6mm (No.4) needles.
Measurements: To fit sizes 10/12/14.
Length: 58/61/64cm (23/24/25in). *Sleeve seam:* 45/46/47cm ($17\frac{1}{2}$/18/$18\frac{1}{2}$in).

Back
With 5.5mm (No.5) needles cast on 59/63/67 sts and work 10 rows K1, P1 rib.
Change to 6mm (No.4) needles and cont as follows:
Next row: (K3,P1) to last 3 sts, K3.
Next and every following row: P the K sts and K the P sts of previous row.
Cont until 16/20/24 rows have been worked from cast on.
Dec 1 st at beg and end of next row.
Work 19 rows.
Repeat the last 20 rows once more (55/59/63 sts).
Shape armholes: Cast off 4 sts at beg of next 2 rows (47/51/55 sts).
Dec 1 st at beg of next and every following row until 41/43/45 sts rem *.
Cont without shaping until 92/96/100 rows have been worked from cast on.
Shape shoulders: Cast off 10/11/12 sts at beg of next 2 rows.
Cast off rem 21 sts.
Front
As back to *.
Cont without shaping until 76/80/84 rows have been worked from cast on, ending with a wrong side row.
Divide for neck: Left side: Next row: Work 15/16/17 sts, turn and slip rem sts on to a stitch holder.
Dec 1 st at beg of next and every following alt row until 10/11/12 sts rem.
Cont without shaping until 92/96/100 rows have been worked from cast on.
Cast off.

Right side: Next row: Rejoin yarn to held sts and cast off centre 11 sts.
Work rem 15/16/17 sts.
Next row: Work to end.
Dec 1 st at beg of next and every following alt row until 10/11/12 sts rem.
Cont without shaping until 93/97/101 rows have been worked from cast on.
Cast off.
Sleeves (2 alike)
With 5.5mm (No.5) needles cast on 31/31/31 sts and work 10 rows K1, P1 rib.
Change to 6mm (No.4) needles and cont as follows:
Next row: (K3, P1) to last 3 sts, K3.
Next and every following row: P the K sts and K the P sts of previous row.
Cont until 16/18/20 rows have been worked from cast on.
Inc 1 st at beg and end of next and every following 8th row until there are 43/43/43 sts on the needle.
Cont without shaping until 70/72/74 rows have been worked from cast on.
Shape sleeve head: Cast off 4 sts at beg of next 2 rows (35 sts).
Dec 1 st at beg of next 2 rows.
Work 2 rows.
Repeat the last 4 rows once more (31 sts).
Dec 1 st at beg of next and every following row until 15 sts rem. Cast off.
Polo neck (all sizes)
Join right shoulder seam. With 5.5mm (No.5) needles and right side facing pick up and K 15 sts down left front neck, 11 sts across centre, 15 sts up right front neck, and 22 sts across back (63 sts).
Work 34 rows K1, P1 rib.
Cast off in rib.
To make up
Press work according to instructions on ball band. Join left shoulder seam and collar. Sew in sleeves. Join side and sleeve seams. Press seams.

Variations
This is such a useful sweater just as it is that variations aren't really necessary, but you could:
a) Knit fewer rows at the neck to make a turtle or crew neck style.
b) Knit the body and sleeves in a fluffy wool and the collar and welts in plain wool.

11 Pin-tucked blouse

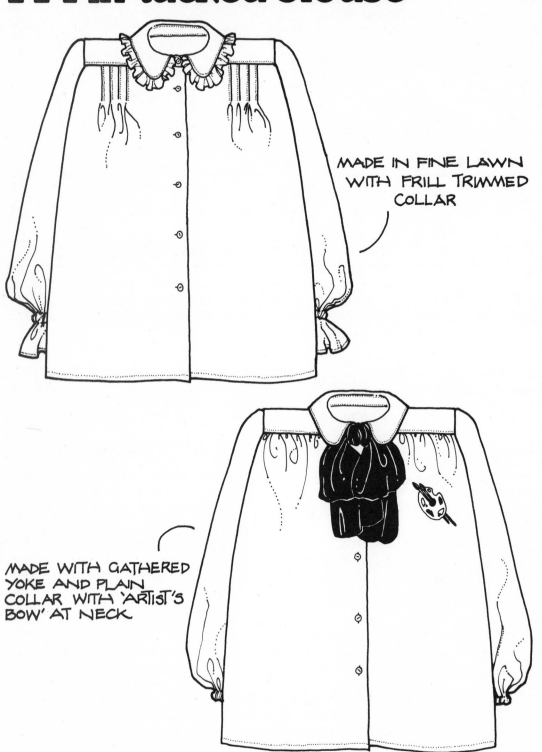

MADE IN FINE LAWN WITH FRILL TRIMMED COLLAR

MADE WITH GATHERED YOKE AND PLAIN COLLAR WITH 'ARTIST'S BOW' AT NECK

48

OPPOSITE: *Ethnic winter dress (page 19)*

Sweetest little blouse with heaps of possibilities. Make it in white, trimmed with lace, for a romantic effect. Or in crisp stripes and checks with a touch of piping for work wear.

Fabric: 2.75m (3yd) of 90cm (36in) wide fabric.
Notions: Stiffening (lightweight) for collar, neckband and front facings; shirring elastic; 6 shirt buttons.

1. Cut collar, collar band and front facings from stiffening.
2. With right sides together, place two collar sections together. Take stiffening collar section and place on top of fabric collar sections.
3. Sew round outside curved edge, leaving long neck edge free. Clip curves and trim seam, turn out and press.
4. Take the two collar band sections and, with right sides together, place one on top of the other. Sandwich the completed collar between them, taking care to match the centre back of both collar and band. Tack through all layers.
5. Take the stiffening collar band and place on top of one fabric band. Pin and then sew all round curved edge of collar band leaving long neck edge free. Trim seam and clip curves, turn out and press well.
6. Pin, tack and sew pin-tucks down to mark indicated on pattern.
7. Trim away seam allowance on both long edges of the two front facings cut from stiffening.
8. Tack stiffening to wrong side of facings, leaving a seam allowance of fabric extending at each side. On outer curved edge of facing fold over the allowance and stitch down close to edge, trim away excess. Repeat on second facing.
9. With right sides together match front facing to blouse front and stitch down straight centre front line. Fold facing back onto inside of blouse and press. Repeat with second facing.
10. With right sides together match the front edges of the two yoke sections, sandwiching the pin-tucked edges of the blouse fronts between them. Stitch through all layers. Trim seams and press.
11. Take back body section and run a line of gathering along the top edge. Draw up gently to fit back edge of yoke.
12. With right sides together, pin gathered raw edge of back to raw edge of top yoke section and sew. Trim seam and press gathers towards inside of yoke.
13. Turn to inside of blouse, turn under and press the remaining raw edge of the yoke and slipstitch down, using previous stitching line as a guide. Topstitch a line close to the yoke seam. (See 'How To' Guide.)
14. With right sides together sew side seams of blouse and press.
15. Tack the front facing (folded back into place) at the neck edge to secure.
16. Take the collar and collar band section and, taking care to match the centre back of the collar with the centre back of the blouse neck, pin one free edge of the collar band to the blouse (with right sides together). Also make sure that the collar band ends match the front edges of the blouse. Sew in place.
17. Trim the seam and clip curves (see 'How To' Guide). Press the seam towards the collar.
18. Turn under and press the remaining free edge of the collar and slipstitch into place using the previous stitching line as a guide.
19. Take sleeve section and with right sides together sew underarm seam and press. Repeat with second sleeve.
20. Turn up, tack and stitch a 6mm ($\frac{1}{4}$in) hem all round sleeve bottom and then tack and stitch a further hem of 1.5cm ($\frac{5}{8}$in). Repeat with second sleeve.
21. Run two lines of shirring around sleeve, 5cm (2in) up from sleeve hem to form flounced cuff. (See 'How To' Guide.)
22. Pin and sew in both sleeves. (See 'How To' Guide.)
23. Open out front facing at blouse hem and turn up and stitch a 6mm ($\frac{1}{4}$in) hem, all round bottom of blouse.

Gathered trousers (page 69) with picture sweater (page 43).   49

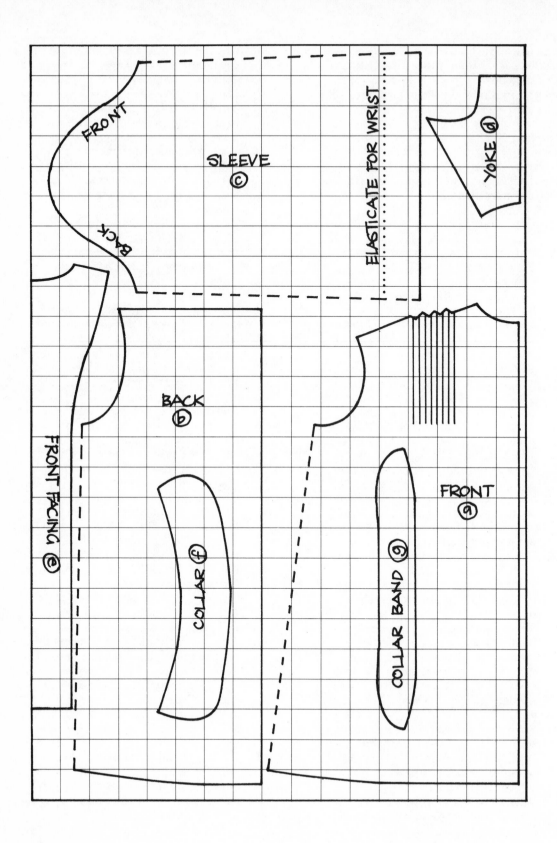

FRONT

SLEEVE ©

ELASTICATE FOR WRIST

YOKE ⓓ

BACK

BACK ⓑ

FRONT FACING ⓔ

COLLAR ⓕ

COLLAR BAND ⓖ

FRONT ⓐ

50

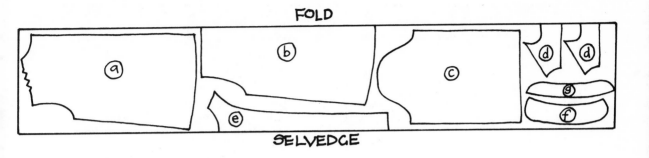

FOLD

SELVEDGE

24. Fold facings back onto blouse (right sides together) and pin. Stitch a line 2cm ($\frac{3}{4}$in) up from hem. Clip front corners, turn out facings and press.
25. Press up hem using stitching line as a guide, then slipstitch or machine stitch down.
26. Mark buttonholes, one on collar band and five spaced evenly down the front. (Use more if you like.)
27. Work buttonholes, sew on buttons and fasten.

Variations

a) This blouse is at its loveliest made in fine white cotton lawn, with a trimming of narrow lace slipstitched on the underside of the collar and around the sleeve hem.

b) For an artist's shirt, make the blouse in crisp cotton check. Instead of the pin-tucks, use gathering, shorten the sleeves by 5cm (2in) and elasticate the cuffs. Finish off with a huge grosgrain ribbon bow.

12 Tailored overshirt

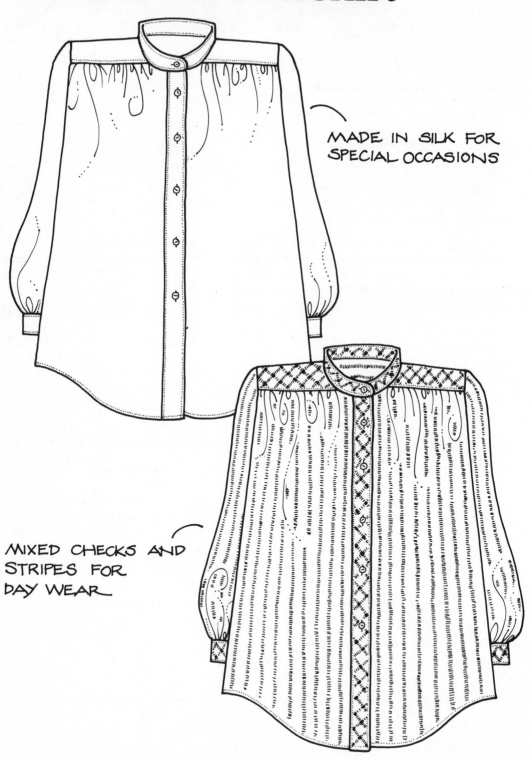

MADE IN SILK FOR
SPECIAL OCCASIONS

MIXED CHECKS AND
STRIPES FOR
DAY WEAR

That vital overshirt, to cover everything that needs covering. Perfect with pants, jeans or even skirts. Nice and easy to wear every single day – to work, around the house, or out and about.

Fabric: 2.85m ($3\frac{1}{8}$yd) of 90cm (36in) wide fabric; stiffening (lightweight) for collar and front bands.
Notions: 9 shirt buttons.

1. Cut a single collar and two front bands from the stiffening.
2. With right sides together place collar sections together and pin. Then place stiffening collar section on top and tack.
3. Sew round curved outer edge through all thicknesses, trim and clip curves (see 'How To' Guide). Turn out and press.
4. Trim the seam allowance from one long side of the front band stiffening. Repeat on second stiffening band.
5. Tack the stiffening to the wrong side of the fabric shirt band. Fold over the excess fabric down one long side and tack, trim and press. Repeat on second front band.
6. Take *right* shirt front and one front band, match right side of raw band edge to wrong side of shirt front and sew.
7. Trim seam right back and press the band onto the right side of the shirt front. Tack into place.
8. Topstitch close to both sides of front band. Take out tacking.
9. Take *left* shirt front and, this time with right sides together, match raw edge of second band with front edge of shirt and sew. Trim seam and press the band back to inside of shirt front. Tack down.
10. Take one shirt front and run a line of gathering along shoulder edge. Draw up gently. Repeat with second front.
11. With right sides together match the two yoke sections, sandwich the two gathered edges of the shirt fronts between them and sew across shoulders. Trim seam and press yoke away from the shirt front.
12. Take back shirt section and run a line of gathering along the top edge, gently draw up. With right sides together pin gathered raw edge of back to raw edge of top yoke section, and sew. Trim and press seam towards yoke.
13. Turn to inside of blouse, fold under and press the seam allowance on the remaining raw edge of the yoke. Slipstitch down using previous stitching line as a guide. Press.
14. Take the collar and, with right sides together, match the centre back of one raw edge (single thickness) of the collar to the outside centre back of the shirt neck. Pin and tack round neck. Sew, trim and clip seam allowance, then press the seam towards the collar.
15. Turn under the 1.5cm ($\frac{5}{8}$in) seam allowance along remaining raw edge of the collar and press. Slipstitch down using the previous sewing line as a guide.
16. Take the sleeve section and with right sides together, sew underarm seam, leaving 5cm (2in) unsewn at the cuff

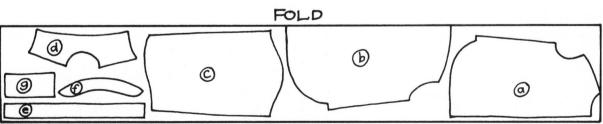

FOLD

SELVEDGE

53

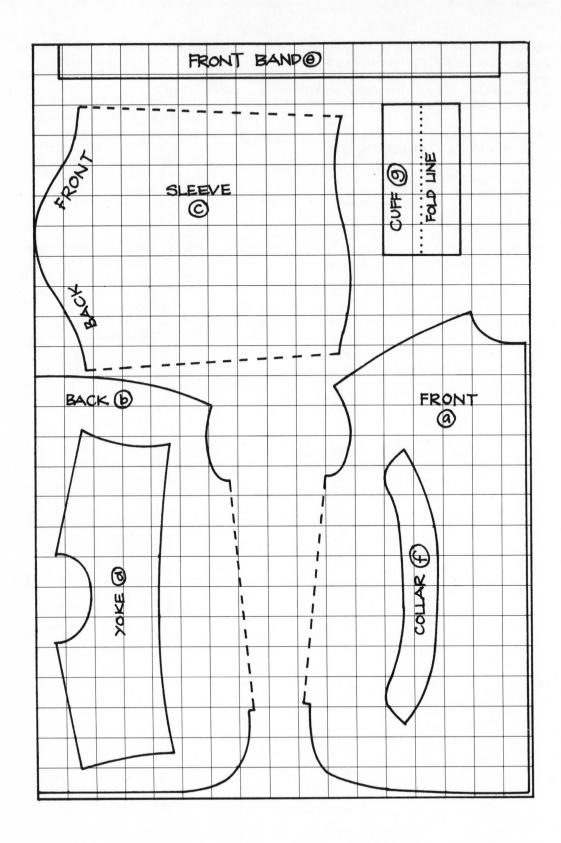

FRONT BAND (e)

FRONT

BACK

SLEEVE (c)

CUFF (g)

FOLD LINE

BACK (b)

FRONT (a)

YOKE (d)

COLLAR (f)

end. Press back the seam allowance at this opening and topstitch all round it. Repeat with second sleeve.

17. Take cuff section and, with right sides together, fold along line indicated on pattern. Sew both short edges, trim seam, turn out and press.

18. Run a line of gathering along bottom of sleeve and draw up, until it measures the same as the cuff. Take one free edge (single thickness) of one cuff and with right sides together, pin and sew to bottom of sleeve. Trim seam and press towards inside of cuff.

19. Turn under and press the seam allowance on remaining free edge of cuff. Slipstitch into place using previous sewing line as a guide. Topstitch around outside edge of cuff. Repeat with second sleeve.

20. With right sides together sew side seams of shirt down to curved edge of hem. Press.

21. Pin in and sew both sleeves (see 'How To' Guide).

22. Neaten hem edge and then turn up and machine a narrow hem all round the shirt bottom.

23. Mark out and work the position of the buttonholes, one on the collar band, six down the front of the shirt and one on each cuff. (Use more if you wish.) Sew on buttons.

Variations

a) This is one of the most useful shirts you can have – wear it over skirts, trousers, knickerbockers and shorts. Wear it under pinafores and waistcoats. It looks great in crisp checks or warm fine wools.

b) For evenings or stylish work days, it looks terrific in silk.

13 Waistcoats

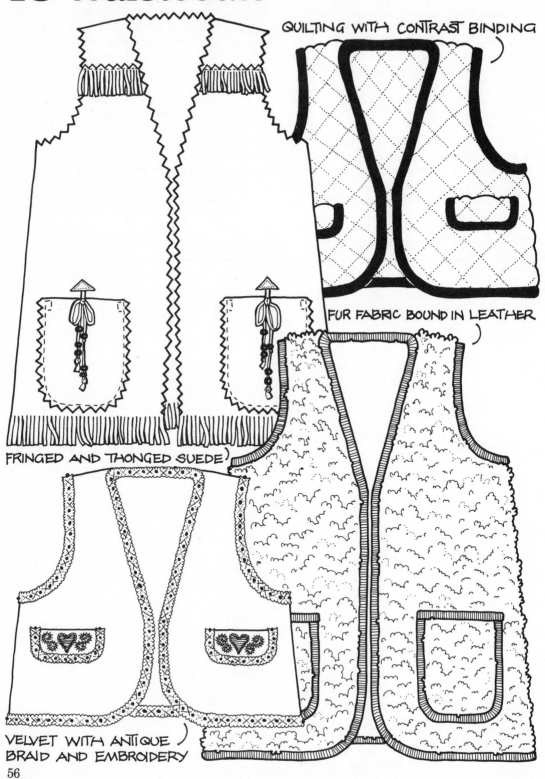

QUILTING WITH CONTRAST BINDING

FUR FABRIC BOUND IN LEATHER

FRINGED AND THONGED SUEDE

VELVET WITH ANTIQUE BRAID AND EMBROIDERY

56

Simple edge to edge waistcoats that perk up dresses, sweaters and shirts. The bound edges are child's play – no nasty facings or fastenings to tackle.

Fabric: *Long waistcoat:* 1.35m (1½yd) of 90cm (36in) wide fabric. *Short waistcoat:* 80cm (⅞yd) of 90cm (36in) wide fabric.
Notions: *Long waistcoat:* 5.00m (5½yd) of bias binding. *Short waistcoat:* 4.00m (4½yd) of bias binding.

1. Mark and sew the back neck darts.
2. With right sides together, match and sew shoulder seams. Fell these seams. (See 'How To' Guide.)

3. To prepare short waistcoat pocket flap, bind curved outside edge (see 'How To' Guide), leaving top edge raw. Then pin into place with the curved edge pointing towards the shoulder line. Stitch across and then press pocket flap down towards hem. Topstitch close to top folded edge to keep flap down.
4. To prepare patch pocket for long waistcoat, first turn over a 2.5cm (1in) hem at pocket top and press. Then bind all round curved outside edge. Pin into place and then topstitch down along inner edge of binding.
5. With right sides together, match and sew side seams and fell them.

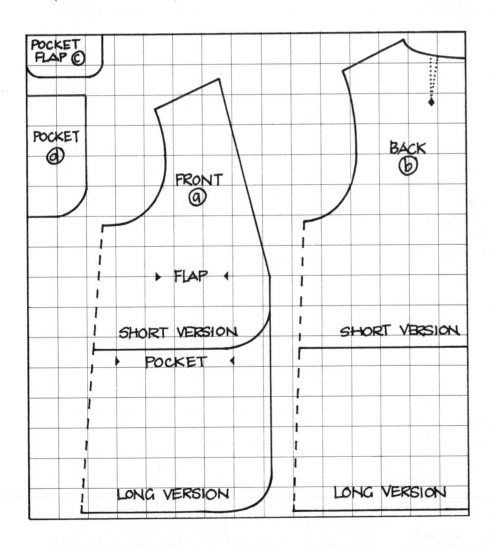

57

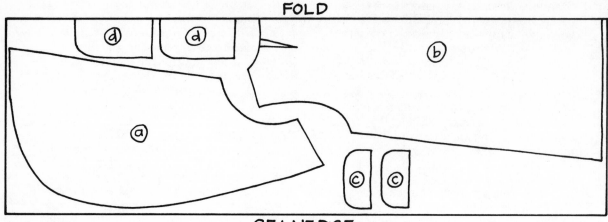

FOLD

SELVEDGE

6. Starting and ending at centre back neck seam, bind all round the waistcoat edge.
7. Starting and ending at underarm seam, bind all round armhole edges.

Variations
a) The long version would look marvellous in suede, trimmed with thongs and beads.
b) Make the short version out of some precious piece of fabric you've been saving for ages, and then hunt round antique and junk shops for some genuine old trimming.

14 Oriental bolero

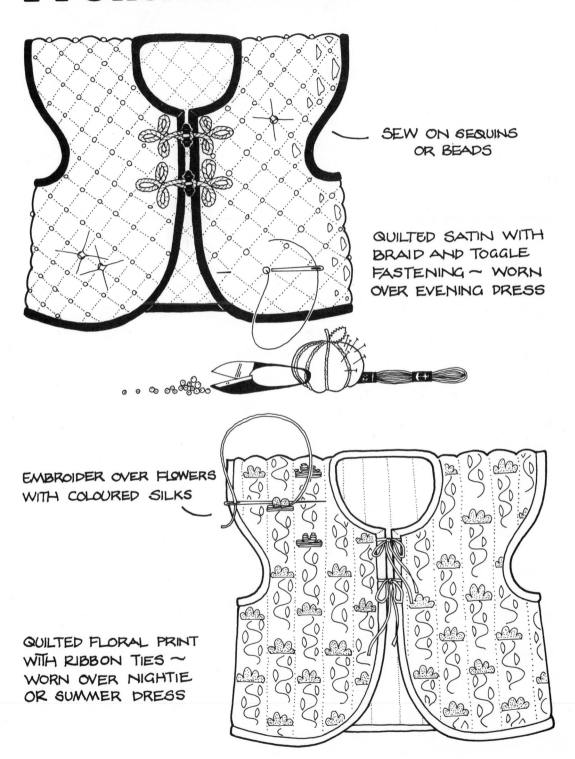

SEW ON SEQUINS OR BEADS

QUILTED SATIN WITH BRAID AND TOGGLE FASTENING ~ WORN OVER EVENING DRESS

EMBROIDER OVER FLOWERS WITH COLOURED SILKS

QUILTED FLORAL PRINT WITH RIBBON TIES ~ WORN OVER NIGHTIE OR SUMMER DRESS

59

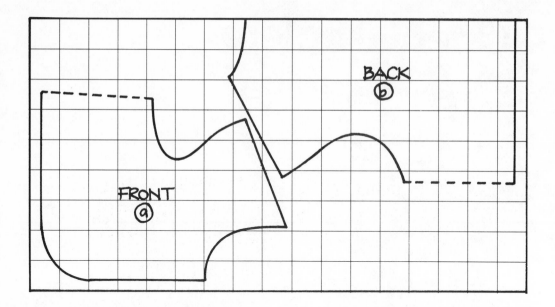

Another really useful little bolero that can wake up the simplest dress or plain shirt. It leads a double life too as a pretty bedjacket.

Fabric: 90cm (1yd) of 90cm (36in) wide quilted fabric.

Notions: 3.75m ($4\frac{1}{8}$yd) of wide bias binding; 2 ready-made frog fastenings.

1. With right sides together, match front and back sections and sew shoulder seams. Fell this seam (see 'How To' Guide).
2. With right sides together match and sew side seams. Fell these seams too.
3. Starting at one centre front neck edge, bind down centre front, round hem and then up second front. (See 'How To' Guide.)
4. Bind neck edge.
5. Starting and ending at underarm seam, bind round armholes.
6. Position frog fastenings and slipstitch into place.

Variations

a) In quilted brocade with satin bias braids, this little bolero would look stunning over a plain evening dress or a silky overshirt.

b) In sprigged cotton quilting, it makes a delicious bedjacket.

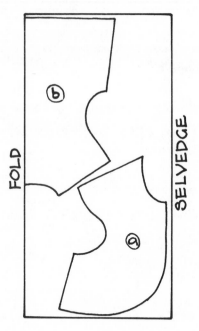

60

TROUSERS & SKIRTS

15 Laced front trousers

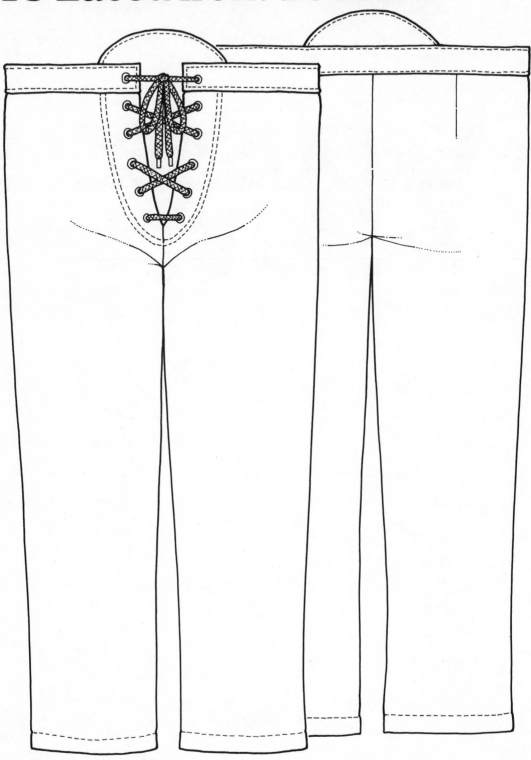

Trousers that fasten in the same way as a pair of plimsolls! Loosen the laces and let the front expand as you do. These look great in denim and heavyweight fabrics to give a super tailored look.

Fabric: 2.25m ($2\frac{1}{2}$yd) of 90cm (36in) wide fabric.
Notions: Iron-on interfacing for waistband and front facings; eyelet and eyelet tool; 2.00m (2yd) of narrow cord to thread through eyelets; small piece of lining for second flap.

1. Cut flap section from lining. Mark eyelet holes on trouser fronts.
2. With right sides together, match fabric and lining flap sections. Sew all round flap, leaving a small gap at the bottom edge to enable you to turn it right side out. Clip and trim the seam allowance, turn out and press. Slipstitch opening together and then topstitch all round flap (see 'How To' Guide).
3. Take the two front facing sections and iron on the interfacing, then neaten round the outside curved edge. With right sides together, stitch up to the mark on the pattern. Clip and press open. Then turn back and press the seam allowance on the same centre front edges. Tack.
4. Take the two trouser front sections and with right sides together, stitch up to mark indicated on pattern. Clip seam and press open. Then fold back the seam allowance on the rest of the centre front seam and press. Tack.
5. With wrong sides together match the front facing to the trouser front opening and tack together round the very edge of the opening and also round the curved edge of the front facing. Press.
6. Now topstitch all round front opening very close to the sandwiched together edges. Then topstitch all round the outside edge of the facing.
7. Attach eyelets according to manufacturer's instructions.
8. Take both back trouser sections, pin and sew darts. Press. With right sides together sew centre back seam. Clip, trim and press.
9. With right sides together, sew both side seams and press.
10. With right sides together and taking care to match centre front and centre back seams, sew inside leg seam from trouser hem to trouser hem. Clip, trim and press seam.
11. Take waistband section and iron interfacing onto wrong side. With right sides together, fold along line indicated on pattern.
12. Sew both short ends, trim and turn out. Press.
13. With right sides together and matching ends of waistband with front edges of trousers, pin one free edge of waistband (single thickness) to trouser waist edge. Tack and sew. Trim, clip and press seam towards band.
14. Turn under seam allowance on remaining free edge of waistband and press. Slipstitch down using previous stitching line as a guide. Then topstitch all round waistband.

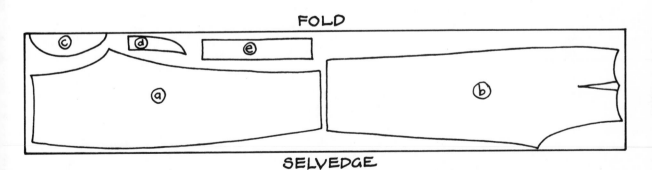

FOLD

SELVEDGE

63

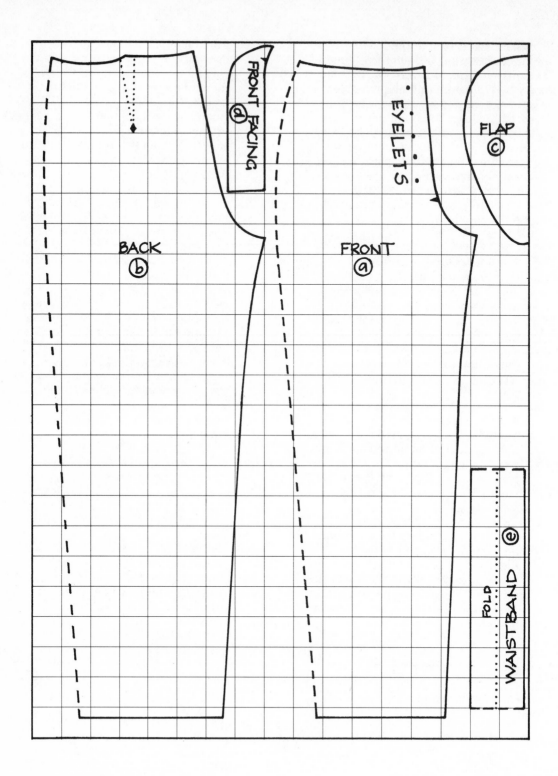

FRONT FACING (d)

FLAP (c)

EYELETS

BACK (b)

FRONT (a)

FOLD

WAISTBAND (e)

15. Mark and attach one further eyelet to each side of the waistband, in line with the eyelets down the front.
16. Take front panel and slipstitch the base of the flap securely to the centre front seam on the inside of the trousers. To hold it more securely you could topstitch through all layers with a few machine stitches.
17. Slot cord through eyelets as you would when lacing a shoe.
18. Try on trousers and hem as desired.

Variations
a) These trousers look great in denim. They have slim-fitting legs, and if you want a more jeans-style look, you can add plenty of topstitching down the seams and around the waistband.
b) They are best suited to heavy fabrics – you can get a really tailored look if you make them in barathea or gabardine.

16 Panel front trousers

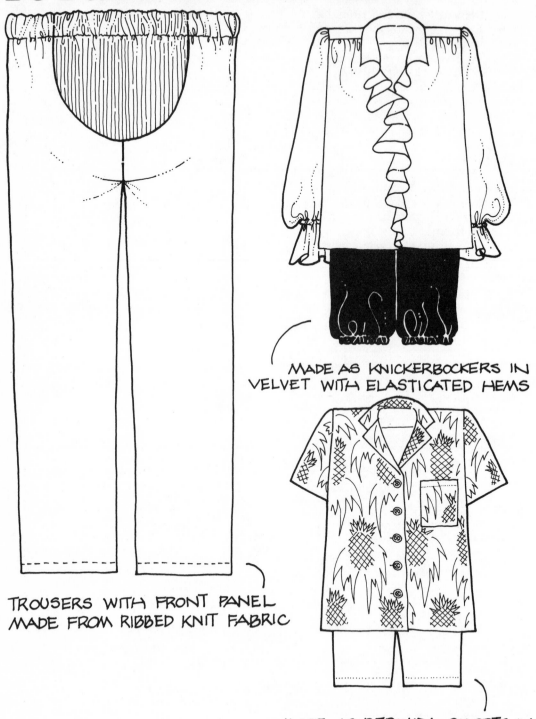

MADE AS KNICKERBOCKERS IN VELVET WITH ELASTICATED HEMS

TROUSERS WITH FRONT PANEL MADE FROM RIBBED KNIT FABRIC

MADE AS BERMUDA SHORTS IN BRIGHT CRISP COTTON

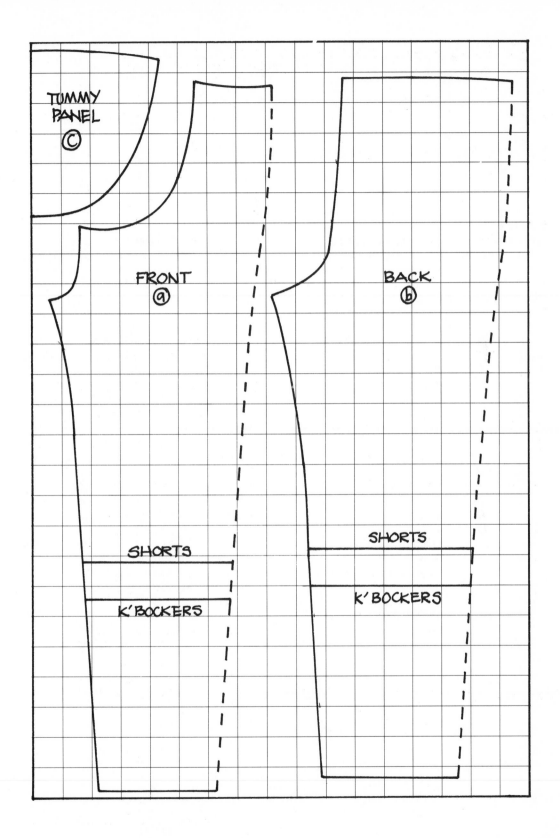

TUMMY PANEL ©

FRONT ⓐ

BACK ⓑ

SHORTS

SHORTS

K'BOCKERS

K'BOCKERS

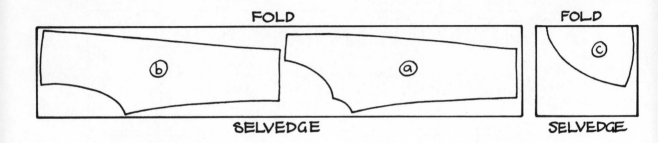

These trousers are suitable for medium weight fabrics, with a comfortable stretch tummy panel. They're easy to make – but don't stop at just trousers. Try some knickerbockers and shorts too!

Fabric: *Basic trousers:* 2.40m ($2\frac{5}{8}$yd) of 90cm (36in) wide fabric. *Knickerbockers:* 1.80m (2yd) of 90cm (36in) wide fabric. *Shorts:* 1.70m ($1\frac{1}{8}$yd) of 90cm (36in) wide fabric.
Notions: 50cm ($\frac{5}{8}$yd) of ribbed jersey-knit fabric (for front panel); 2.5cm (1in) wide elastic.

1. Take the two back sections and with right sides together, sew centre back seam from waist to crotch. Trim, clip and press.
2. Take the two front sections and with right sides together sew the short centre front seam. Trim, clip and press.
3. Take the ribbed jersey tummy panel and with right sides together carefully pin into place. Sew, trim seam and neaten.
4. With right sides together place front and back sections together and sew side seams. Press seams.
5. With right sides together sew inside leg seams in one, from trouser hem to trouser hem, making sure to match front and back centre seams.
6. Turn over and sew a 6mm ($\frac{1}{4}$in) hem all round the top of the trousers, then turn over a further 4cm ($1\frac{1}{2}$in) hem and stitch round close to the edge leaving a small gap at the centre back through which to slot the elastic.
7. Sew a second line of stitching close to the topmost edge of the trousers. This forms a neat channel for the elastic.
8. Try on trousers and turn up hem as desired.

Variations
a) This is a marvellously useful pair of trousers suitable for medium weight fabrics like wool and all kinds of jersey.
b) What about ringing the changes with a high fashion pair of knickerbockers? Teamed with thick-knit tights and boots they make a terrific addition to your wardrobe. Make them in needlecord or checked wool and wear them with a chunky-knit sweater and a swirly cape. Simply elasticate the legs in the same way as the waist.
c) Who says pregnant ladies can't wear shorts? These bermudas have a crisply tailored look and are smashing for summer.

17 Gathered trousers and jumpsuit

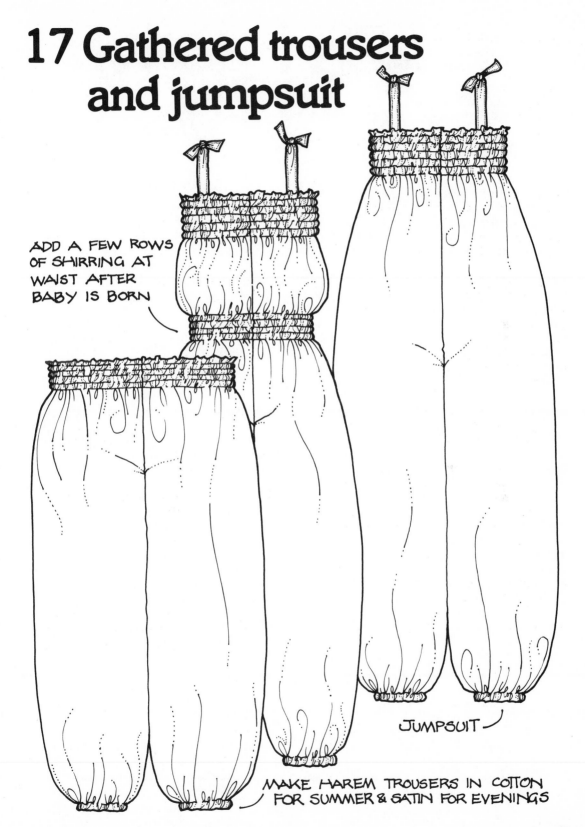

ADD A FEW ROWS OF SHIRRING AT WAIST AFTER BABY IS BORN

JUMPSUIT

MAKE HAREM TROUSERS IN COTTON FOR SUMMER & SATIN FOR EVENINGS

69

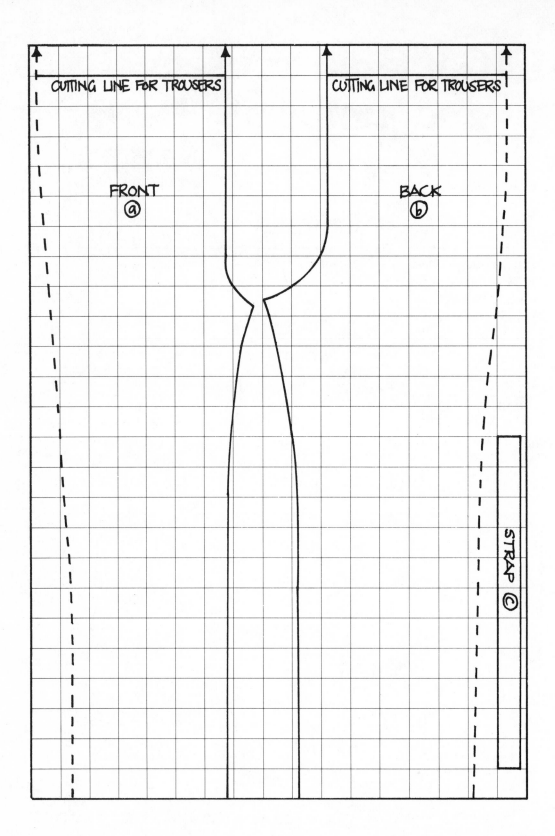

CUTTING LINE FOR TROUSERS

FRONT
ⓐ

CUTTING LINE FOR TROUSERS

BACK
ⓑ

STRAP ©

70

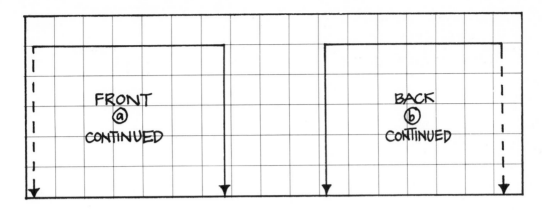

FRONT ⓐ CONTINUED

BACK ⓑ CONTINUED

FOLD

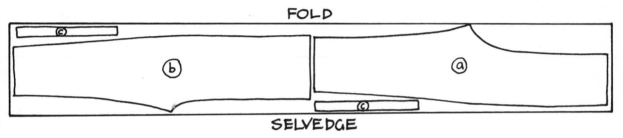

ⓑ ⓐ ©

SELVEDGE

Even the novice dressmaker can tackle these trousers with confidence – they simply couldn't be easier. They are best made in lightweight fabric for both day and evening. And simply by extending the pattern you can make a snazzy jumpsuit. With a little more work you can go on wearing it after baby has arrived.

Trousers

Fabric: 2.40m ($2\frac{5}{8}$yd) of 90cm (36in) wide fabric.

Notions: Shirring elastic; 6mm ($\frac{1}{4}$in) wide elastic for hems.

1. Take two front sections and with right sides together, sew centre front seam from waist to crotch. Press and neaten.
2. Repeat with two back sections.
3. Take front and back sections and with right sides together, sew side seams. Press and neaten.
4. With right sides together sew inside leg seam from trouser hem to trouser hem, taking care to match front and back centre seams. Press.

5. Turn over and tack a 6mm ($\frac{1}{4}$in) hem all round trouser top, then turn over and stitch a further 13mm ($\frac{1}{2}$in) hem all round top edge. Press.
6. Then, making complete circuits of the waist, machine five or six rows of shirring 1.5cm ($\frac{5}{8}$in) down from top edge, starting and ending at centre back seam. (See 'How To' Guide.)
7. Turn up and sew a 6mm ($\frac{1}{4}$in) hem all round trouser leg hems, then turn up a further 1.5cm ($\frac{5}{8}$in) hem all round, leaving a small gap through which to insert elastic.
8. Slot elastic through trouser hems, draw up to fit and sew securely.

Jumpsuit

Fabric: 3.00m ($3\frac{3}{8}$yd) of 90cm (36in) wide fabric.

Notions: Shirring elastic; 6mm ($\frac{1}{4}$in) wide elastic for hems.

Sew in exactly the same way as for gathered trousers. Then:

9. Take the four strap sections and make four flat straps. (See 'How To' Guide.)

71

10. Try on jumpsuit and pin straps in place. Then slipstitch them securely to inside of suit using shirring lines as a guide. Tie straps in bows on your shoulders.

Variations
a) These softly gathered trousers are best made in fine cloth such as lightweight cotton, cheesecloth or voile.
b) Equally, they look terrific for evenings in fine crêpe or satin.
c) The jumpsuit made in brightly coloured cotton is ideal for holidays or even pottering about in the garden.
d) After baby is born, run a few more lines of shirring around the jumpsuit waist and you can keep right on wearing it.

Tailored overshirt (page 52) with laced-front trousers (page 62).

18 Painter's overalls

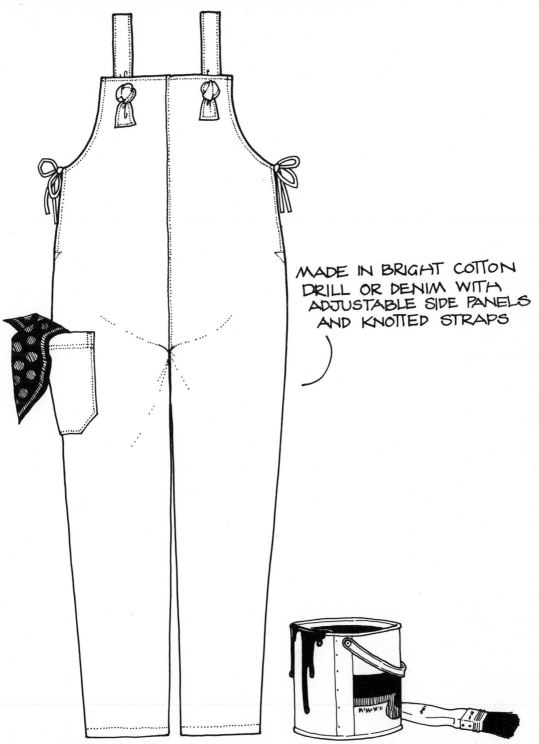

MADE IN BRIGHT COTTON DRILL OR DENIM WITH ADJUSTABLE SIDE PANELS AND KNOTTED STRAPS

Painter's overalls (page 73) and gathered dungarees (page 69).

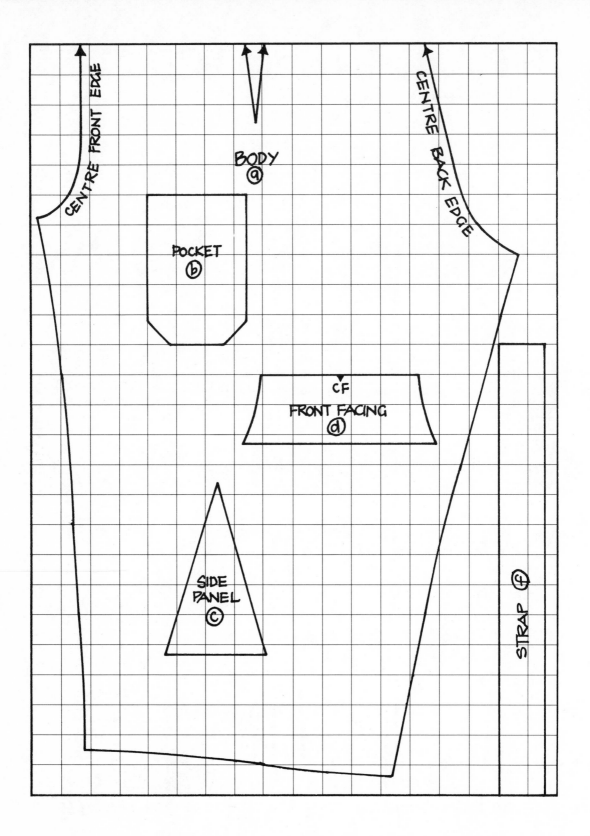

CENTRE FRONT EDGE

CENTRE BACK EDGE

BODY
ⓐ

POCKET
ⓑ

CF
FRONT FACING
ⓓ

SIDE
PANEL
ⓒ

STRAP ⓕ

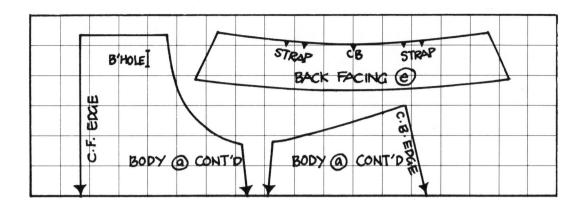

Based on a traditional painter's overall, these dungarees really are great. They fit everyone and they come in handy after baby is born for wearing around the home for housework or decorating.

Sizes: One size fits sizes 10 to 14.
Fabric: 4.00m ($4\frac{1}{2}$yd) of 90cm (36in) wide fabric.
Notions: 1m (1yd) of narrow webbing in a toning colour.

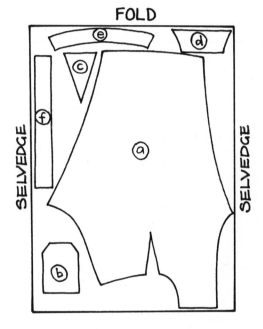

1. Take one trouser section and with right sides together pin in and sew the V-shaped side panel. Neaten seam with oversewing and press. Repeat with second section and panel.

2. Take pocket section and with right sides together, fold over flap and stitch down at each side. Clip corners, turn out and press. Turn over and press seam allowance all round rest of pocket. Pin in place and topstitch down.

3. With right sides together match centre front seam. Sew, fell (see 'How To' Guide), and press.

4. With right sides together match centre back seam and sew, fell and press.

5. With right sides together and taking care to match centre front and back seams, sew the inside leg seam from trouser hem to trouser hem.

6. Take a strap section and with right sides together sew up one long side and across straight short side. Turn out and press, then topstitch all round. Repeat with second strap.

7. With right sides together match straps to marks at dungaree back and tack in place to outside of fabric with the straps hanging down towards the trouser hems.

8. Take back facing and tack under the seam allowance along long bottom edge and sides, sew. Then with right sides together match remaining raw edge of facing to top edge of dungarees back and stitch, sandwiching the straps between the layers. Turn facing to inside and press then slipstitch to side seams.

75

9. Take the bib facing and turn up the seam allowance along the bottom edge, stitch down and press. Then with right sides together match bib facing to bib of trousers and sew. Turn out and press.
10. Then turn over and tack a hem between bib facing and back facing.
11. Topstitch all round top edge of dungarees stitching down both hems and facings.
12. Cross straps at back and stitch through where they cross.
13. Take the webbing and cut into four equal lengths, topstitch down, one on each side of the two side panels about 5cm (2in) down from top edge.
14. Work buttonholes on each side of bib.
15. Try on dungarees, slot straps through buttonholes and tie, then turn up hems as desired.

Variations
a) Best made in something pretty tough like cotton drill, and in plain bright colours.
b) For a fun party outfit in late pregnancy run them up in dazzling madras checks or full blown chintzes.

19 Two gathered skirts

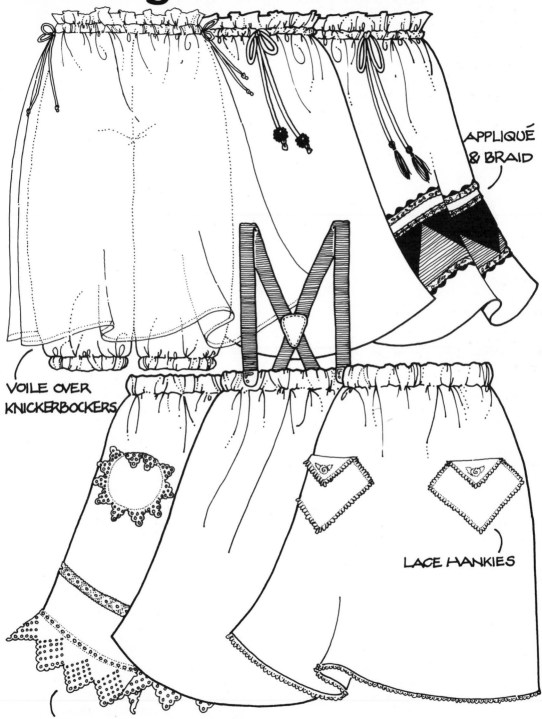

APPLIQUÉ & BRAID

VOILE OVER KNICKERBOCKERS

LACE HANKIES

LACE TABLECLOTH & DOILEY POCKET

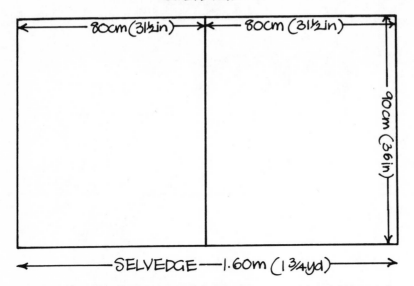

SELVEDGE

| ← 80cm (31½in) → | ← 80cm (31½in) → |
90cm (36in)

← SELVEDGE — 1.60m (1¾yd) →

Another ideal pattern for the beginner. There's no pattern to draft, minimal sewing and it's easy to wear too – what more can you ask? For the more experienced needlewoman, we show lots of ways to add more individual touches.

Lace-trimmed elasticated skirt
Sizes: One size fits sizes 10 to 14.
Fabric: 1.60m ($1\frac{3}{4}$yd) of 90cm (36in) wide fabric.
Notions: 2.5cm (1in) wide elastic; 1.75 (2yd) of narrow lace; two lace-trimmed hankies to match skirt fabric (for pockets).

1. Take two skirt sections and with right sides together, sew side seams. Press seams open.
2. Turn over and sew a 6mm ($\frac{1}{4}$in) hem all round top of skirt, then turn over a further 4cm ($1\frac{1}{2}$in) hem and stitch down, leaving a small gap at one side seam to insert elastic.
3. Sew a further line of stitching around top edge of skirt, to form a neat casing for the elastic.
4. Position pockets as shown in the illustration. Place them diagonally on skirt, stitch the two sides and let the top fall back to form a flap.
5. Insert elastic through waist channel,

draw up to fit and stitch to secure.
6. Try on skirt and adjust hem. Pin and sew.
7. Slipstitch lace to underside of skirt hem.

Drawstring skirt
Sizes: One size fits sizes 10 to 14.
Fabric: 1.80m (2yd) of 90cm (36in) wide fabric.

1. Take one skirt section and mark centre. (This is now the front section.)
2. On right side of fabric, mark and work two vertical buttonholes 1.5cm ($\frac{5}{8}$in) long. They should be placed 1.5cm ($\frac{5}{8}$in) either side of the centre front line, and 4.5 cm ($1\frac{3}{4}$in) down from top edge.
3. Take both skirt sections and with right sides together, sew side seams. Press seams open.
4. Turn over and tack a 1cm ($\frac{1}{2}$in) hem and press. Then turn over a further 3cm ($1\frac{1}{4}$in) hem. Tack and press.
5. Sew two lines of stitching around top of skirt, level with the top and bottom of the buttonholes. This forms a channel for the drawstring.
6. Join the three drawstring sections together at the short ends, forming a long strip. Then sew into a flat tie (see 'How To' Guide).

78

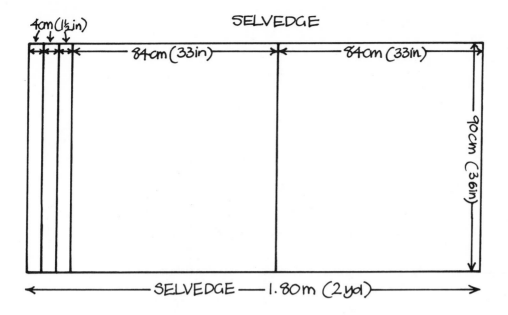

SELVEDGE

4cm (1½in)

84cm (33in) — 84cm (33in)

90cm (36in)

SELVEDGE — 1.80m (2yd)

7. Slot the drawstring through the channel and out through the buttonholes. Draw up and tie in a bow.
8. Try on skirt and hem as desired.

Variations
Elasticated skirt
a) Patch together pieces from an old linen tablecloth to the required size, making a feature of any pretty embroidered edging. As a bonus, use matching circular tablemats for the pockets.
b) Make the skirt in heavyweight brushed cotton check teamed with brightly coloured men's braces (with a clip or button fastening).

Drawstring skirt
a) Make a glamorous, diaphanous evening skirt:
1. Leaving the two sections separate, sew a tiny hem down both side edges of each section. Press.

2. Turn over a 6mm ($\frac{1}{4}$in) hem at top edge and sew. Then turn over a second hem of 4cm ($1\frac{1}{2}$in), and sew.
3. Stitch a line straight across, very close to the top edge of one section, then another line 1.5cm ($\frac{5}{8}$in) down from that.
4. Repeat all this on second skirt section.
5. Using only two of the drawstring pieces, make two flat straps (see 'How To' Guide), then slot one strap through each section.
6. Draw up and tie a bow at each side of your waist, turn up hem as desired.

This skirt looks marvellous over opaque, brightly coloured footless tights or even a swimsuit in summer.

b) For a dramatic, ethnic look, before making up the basic drawstring skirt mark out some bold patterns and appliqué onto the skirt (see 'How To' Guide). Use rich dark colours outlined with gold thread, plus lots of old braid for a real folklore look.

JACKETS & CAPE

20 Bouclé jacket

KNITTED IN HEAVY COTTON WITH POCKET FLAPS OMITTED AND NECK TIED

KNITTED IN TWEEDY YARN

HORN BUTTONS

KNITTED IN BOUCLE

Cosy, swingy jacket worked in unusual quick-growing bouclé yarn – bulky for warmth yet amazingly light to wear. This really is a most versatile jacket, smart enough for work and yet comfortably casual when teamed with shirts and jeans.

Yarn: Of bouclé yarn: 24/25/26 x 50g balls, plus four 2.5cm (1in) buttons.
Needles: A pair of 7mm (No.2).
Tension: 10 sts and 16 rows to 10cm (4in) square, measured over g.st on 7mm (No.2) needles using double thickness of yarn.
Measurements: To fit sizes 10/12/14.
Length: 68/71/74cm (27/28/29in). *Sleeve seam* (when turned back): 45/46/47cm ($17\frac{1}{2}$/18/$18\frac{1}{2}$in).

IMPORTANT: YARN USED DOUBLE THROUGHOUT

Back
With 7mm (No.2) needles cast on 53/56/59 sts and cont in g.st.
Work 22/26/30 rows.
Dec 1 st at beg and end of next row.
Work 15 rows.
Repeat the last 16 rows two more times (47/50/53 sts).
Shape armholes: Cast off 3 sts at beg of next 2 rows (41/44/47 sts).
Dec 1 st at beg of next and every following row until 35/38/41 sts rem.
Cont without shaping until 108/112/116 rows have been worked from cast on.
Shape shoulders: Cast off 10/11/12 sts at beg of next 2 rows.
Cast off rem 15/16/17 sts.
Right front
With 7mm (No.2) needles cast on 25/27/29 sts and cont in g.st.
Work 23/27/31 rows.
Dec 1 st at beg of next row.
Work 15 rows.
Repeat the last 16 rows two more times (22/24/26 sts).
Shape armhole: Next row: Cast off 3 sts, K to end (19/21/23 sts).
Next row: K.
Dec 1 st at beg of next and every following alt row until 17/18/19 sts rem.
Cont without shaping until 82/86/90 rows

have been worked from cast on.
Shape collar: Dec 1 st at beg of next and every following alt row until 10/11/12 sts rem.
Cont without shaping until 109/113/117 rows have been worked from cast on.
Cast off.
Left front
With 7mm (No.2) needles cast on 25/27/29 sts and cont in g.st.
Work 22/26/30 rows.
Dec 1 st at beg of next row.
Work 15 rows.
Repeat the last 16 rows two more times (22/24/26 sts).
Shape armhole: Next row: Cast off 3 sts, K to end.
Next row: K.
Dec 1 st at beg of next and every following alt row until 17/18/19 sts rem.
Cont without shaping until 81/85/89 rows have been worked from cast on.
Shape collar: Dec 1 st at beg of next and every following alt row until 10/11/12 sts rem.
Cont without shaping until 108/112/116 rows have been worked from cast on.
Cast off.
Sleeves (2 alike)
With 7mm (No.2) needles cast on 37/37/37 sts and cont in g.st.
Work 82/84/86 rows.
Shape sleeve head: Cast off 3 sts at beg of next 2 rows (31/31/31 sts).
Dec 1 st at beg of next 2 rows.
K 2 rows.
Repeat the last 4 rows four more times (21 sts).
Dec 1 st at beg of next and every following row until 13 sts rem.
Cast off.
Pockets (2 alike)
With 7mm (No.2) needles cast on 13 sts and cont in g.st.
Work 26 rows.
Dec 1 st at beg of next and every following row until 3 sts rem.
Next row: sl 1, K2 tog, PSSO, break yarn and draw through loop.

To make up
Press work according to instructions on ball band. Join shoulder seams. Sew in sleeves. Join side and sleeve seams,

reversing seam at base of sleeves where the cuff turns back. Position and sew on pockets. Fold back collar. Sew buttons on collar and pockets.

Variations
a) Swap the bouclé yarn for something more tweedy, adding real horn buttons – they are expensive but you only need four.
b) Knit in thick disch-cloth cotton and instead of turning back the collar add long crochet ties.

21 Windcheater jacket

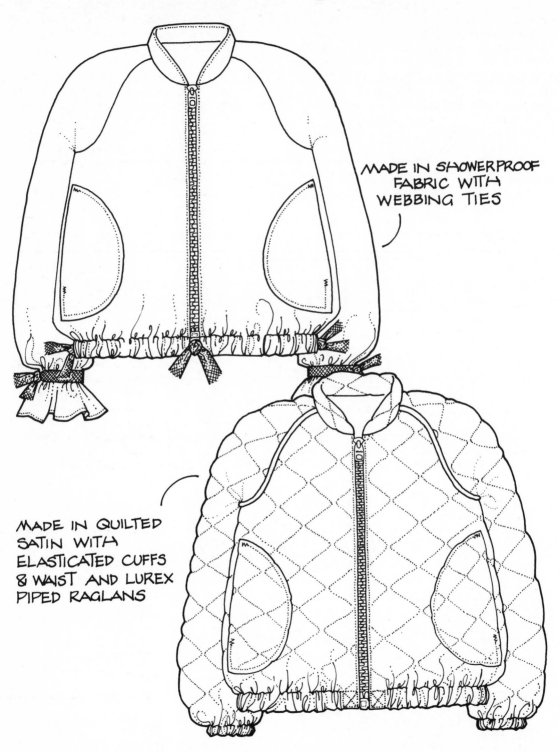

MADE IN SHOWERPROOF FABRIC WITH WEBBING TIES

MADE IN QUILTED SATIN WITH ELASTICATED CUFFS & WAIST AND LUREX PIPED RAGLANS

A real jacket for all seasons. Make it in wool, cotton corduroy or rainproof fabric. You could even make it for evenings. It zips up to a snug-fitting collar, and the hem and cuffs tie with webbing so they will fit comfortably as your waistline grows.

Fabric: 2.00m ($2\frac{1}{4}$yd) of 115cm (45in) wide fabric.
Notions: Stiffening for collar band; 55cm (22in) open-end zip; 4.00m ($4\frac{1}{2}$yd) of 2.5cm (1in) wide webbing.

1. Cut a single collar section from stiffening. With right sides together match and pin the straight edges of the fabric collar sections together. Take the stiffening collar section and place that on top. Tack through all layers. Stitch together along straight edge. Press seam open and trim.
2. Take the front sections and turn over a 1.5cm ($\frac{5}{8}$in) turning down both centre front edges. Tack and press.
3. Take the pocket section and turn over and tack a 1.5cm ($\frac{5}{8}$in) hem all round. Press and tack. Then stitch a line of topstitching (see 'How To' Guide) all round the pocket 1.5cm ($\frac{5}{8}$in) away from the edge.
4. Pin pocket onto jacket and topstitch down very close all round the curved outside edge and approximately 9cm ($3\frac{1}{2}$in) up the straight edge of the pocket from the bottom. Fasten off

securely, take out any tacking and press.
5. Pin and tack closed zip under centre front edges 2cm ($\frac{3}{4}$in) down from neck edge. Sew in zip, take out tacking.
6. Take sleeve section and mark, pin and sew the dart. Press open. Repeat with second sleeve.
7. Take one sleeve section and with right sides together, match points A and B on jacket front to points A and B on sleeve front. Sew between these two points, neaten and press. Repeat with second sleeve and jacket front.
8. Repeat this with sleeve backs and jacket backs.
9. Turn up and sew a 6mm ($\frac{1}{4}$in) hem on jacket back and on both front sections.
10. With right sides together and taking care to match underarm seams, sew from cuff right down underarm and side seam stopping 6cm ($2\frac{1}{4}$in) from the jacket hem. For the last 6cm ($2\frac{1}{4}$in), turn under seam allowances separately, and topstitch down. Repeat on second side.
11. Turn up and press a 6mm ($\frac{1}{4}$in) hem round both sleeve hems. Try on jacket and turn up these hems just slightly longer than normal (just below your wrist bone). Slipstitch down.
12. Turn up a 3cm ($1\frac{1}{4}$in) hem across bottom of jacket back, and across both front sections.
13. Take collar section and trim away the

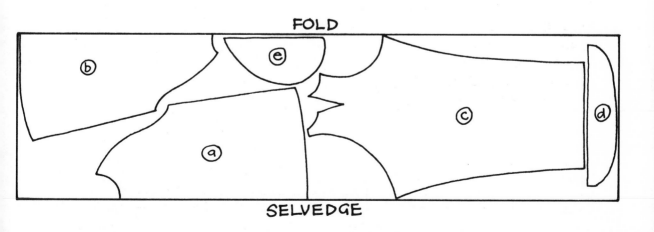

FOLD

SELVEDGE

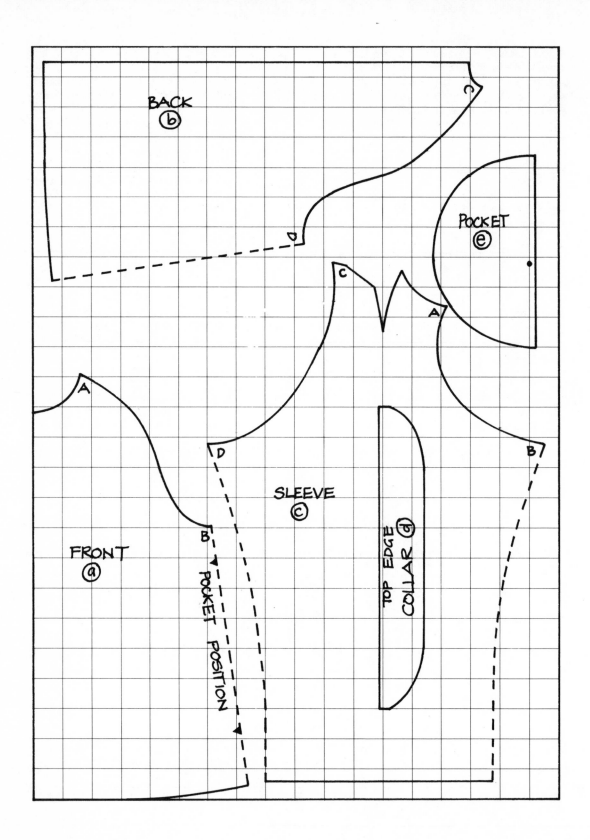

BACK ⓑ

POCKET ⓔ

SLEEVE ©

FRONT ⓐ

POCKET POSITION

TOP EDGE COLLAR ⓓ

seam allowance round long curved edge of the stiffening layer. Fold over and press the excess fabric back onto the stiffening. Tack this in place.

14. With right sides together and taking care to match the centre of the remaining raw edge of the collar section to the centre back of the jacket neckline, pin and stitch the collar onto the jacket – making sure that the collar ends and the jacket fronts match exactly.

15. Fold the collar along seam line to the inside of the jacket and slipstitch it into place using the previous stitching line as a guide.

16. Cut a piece of webbing 1.50m ($1\frac{5}{8}$yd) long and slot it through the bottom hem of the jacket back. Draw up slightly.

17. Cut two further sections of webbing 75cm (29in) long and slot one piece

through each front section, draw up slightly. Tie in bows at side seams and centre front.

18. Cut two further pieces of webbing 50cm ($19\frac{1}{2}$in) long. Fold one piece in half to find the centre point and stitch this point to the underarm seam (on right side of fabric) 6.5cm ($2\frac{1}{2}$in) up from the sleeve hem. Tie round the wrist, forming a cuff. Repeat with second piece of webbing.

Variations

a) For autumn and winter make this roomy jacket in corduroy or tweedy wool.

b) Showerproof poplin is great for warding off springtime rain.

c) You can even make it for evenings too – this time elasticate the hem and sleeves and sew some glittery piping into the raglan seams.

22 Cape

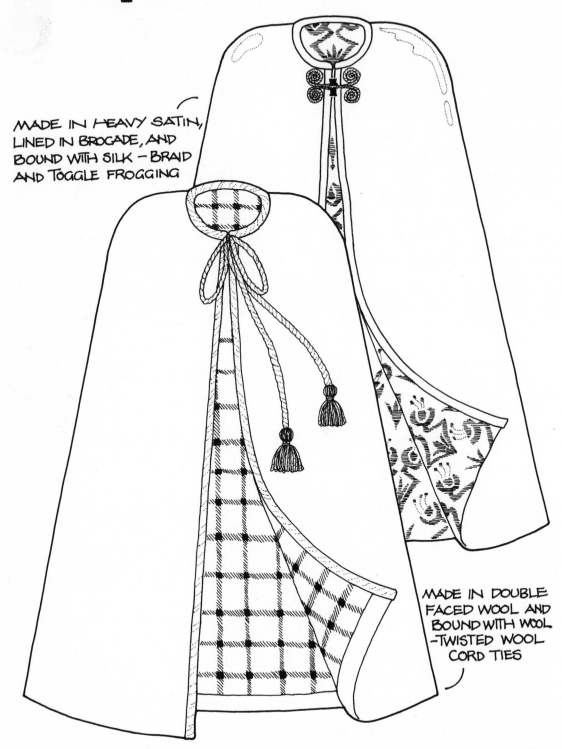

MADE IN HEAVY SATIN,
LINED IN BROCADE, AND
BOUND WITH SILK — BRAID
AND TOGGLE FROGGING

MADE IN DOUBLE
FACED WOOL AND
BOUND WITH WOOL
—TWISTED WOOL
CORD TIES

88   *Gathered skirt (page 77) with pin-tucked blouse (page 48) and bouclé jacket (page 81).*

Wonderfully dramatic cape, less daunting to make than a coat and it keeps you just as warm and dry. Make it in double-faced wool to give you two different looks, or in something glamorous for evenings. You can line it or not, just as you wish, and trim it in any way you choose.

Sizes: One size fits sizes 10 to 14.
Fabric: 3.40m ($3\frac{3}{4}$yd) of 115cm (45in) wide fabric.
Notions: 5.00m ($5\frac{1}{2}$yd) of folded wool braid.

1. Take two back sections and with right sides together, sew back seam and fell it. (See 'How To' Guide.)
2. With right sides together sew side seams and fell.
3. Neaten hem edge and turn up as required.
4. Cut two lengths of wool braid 1.25m ($1\frac{3}{8}$yd) long and bind both front edges. (See 'How To' Guide.)

5. Take the remaining 2.50m ($2\frac{3}{4}$yd) of wool braid and mark the centre of it.
6. Match the centre of the braid to the centre back seam of the cape and bind neck. The remaining braid at each front neck edge must be stitched together along its open edge to form ties.

Variations
a) Capes are ideal cold weather wear. Make one in double-faced wool and you'll have two for the price of one adding valuable mileage to your wardrobe. For a bit more panache, add woolly tassels to the ties.
b) Lightweight showerproof fabric makes an excellent wet weather cape.
c) For evenings make it in a dark fabric lined with something exotic – it's really easy. Simply make up two capes (one from the outer fabric and one from the lining) up to stage 3 in the instructions. Then place the two capes together (wrong sides together) and bind in the same way, but instead of front ties use frog fastenings.

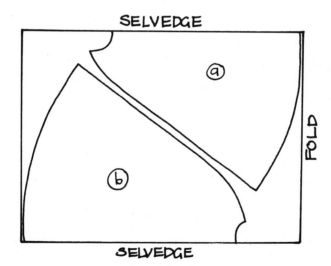

(For pattern pieces, see overleaf.)

Kimono (page 112) and nightdress (page 107) with bedjacket (page 110). 89

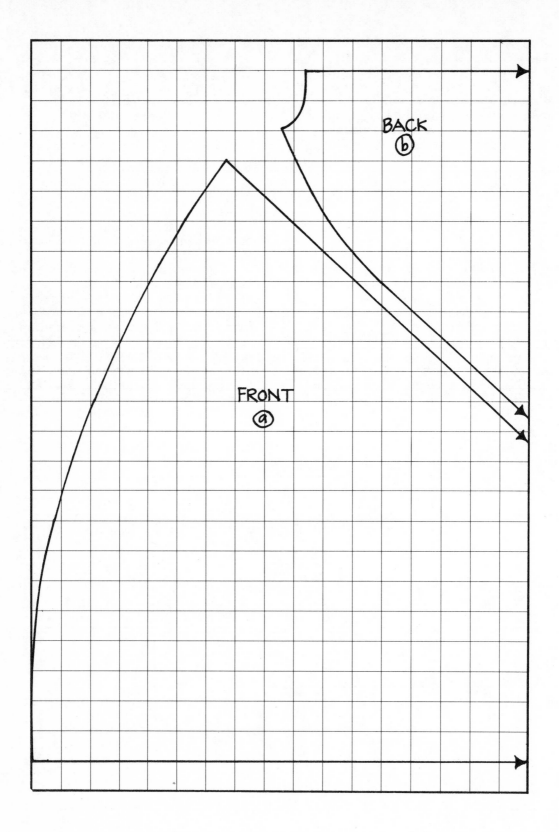

BACK
ⓑ

FRONT
ⓐ

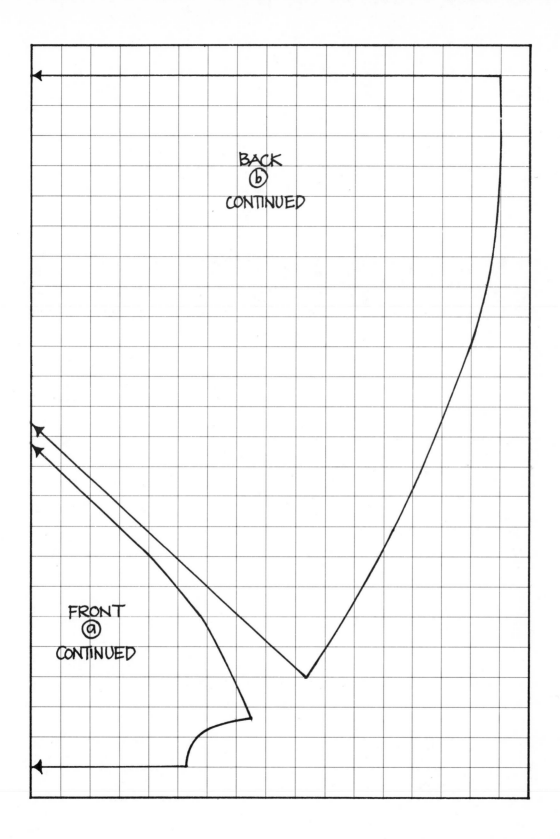

BACK
ⓑ
CONTINUED

FRONT
ⓐ
CONTINUED

SPORTSWEAR

23 Balloon dress and leg warmers

COMBINE DIFFERENT YARNS

MAKE SHORTER AS A SWEATER

Fun knitted dress with matching leg warmers – amazingly warm, cosy and comfortable. Speedy to knit, easy to wear.

Yarn: Of Aran-style yarn (A) 10/10/10 x 50g balls; of heavyweight Chunky-style yarn (B) 16/16/17 x 100g balls.
Needles: A pair each of 9mm (No.00), 7mm (No.2) and 4mm (No.8).
Tension: 8 sts and 10 rows to 10cm (4in) square, measured over st.st on 9mm (No.00) needles using heavyweight yarn.
Measurements: To fit sizes 10/12/14.
Length: 109/112/115cm (43/44/45in).
Sleeve seam: 45/46/47cm (17½/18/18½in).
Legwarmers: 68cm (27in).

Back
With 7mm (No.2) needles and 2 strands of A cast on 44/46/48 sts and work 16 rows K1, P1 rib.
Change to 9mm (No.00) needles and B and cont in st.st comm with a K row.
Cont until 64/66/68 rows have been worked from cast on.
Dec 1 st at beg and end of next row.
Work 9 rows.
Rep the last 10 rows two more times (38/40/42 sts).
Shape armholes: Cast off 2 sts at beg of next 2 rows (34/36/38 sts).
Dec 1 st at beg of next and every following row until 30/30/30 sts rem *.
Cont without shaping until 116/118/120 rows have been worked from cast on.
Shape shoulders: Cast off 8/8/8 sts at beg of next 2 rows. Cast off rem 14 sts.
Front
As back to *.
Cont without shaping until 106/108/110 rows have been worked from cast on, ending with a wrong side row.
Divide for neck: Left side: Next row: K11/11/11, turn and slip rem sts on to a stitch holder.
Dec 1 st at beg of next and every following alt row until 8/8/8 sts rem.
Cont without shaping until 116/118/120 rows have been worked from cast on.
Cast off.
Right side: Next row: Rejoin yarn to held sts, cast off centre 8 sts, K rem 11/11/11 sts.
Next row: P.

Dec 1 st at beg of next and every following alt row until 8/8/8 sts rem.
Cont without shaping until 117/119/121 rows have been worked from cast on.
Cast off.
Sleeves (2 alike)
With 7mm (No.2) needles and 2 strands of A cast on 26/26/26 sts and work 16 rows K1, P1 rib.
Change to 9mm (No.00) needles and B and cont in st.st, comm with a K row.
Work 8/10/12 rows.
Inc 1 st at beg and end of next and following 10th row (30/30/30 sts).
Cont without shaping until 52/54/56 rows have been worked from cast on.
Shape sleeve head: Cast off 2 sts at beg of next 2 rows (26/26/26 sts).
Dec 1 st at beg of next and every following row until 14 sts rem.
Dec 1 st at beg and end of next two rows (10 sts).
Cast off.
Polo collar (all sizes)
Join right shoulder seam. With 7mm (No.2) needles, 2 strands of A, and right side facing pick up and K12 sts down left front neck, 10 sts across centre, 12 sts up right front neck, and 18 sts across back (52 sts). Work 34 rows K1, P1 rib.
Cast off in rib.
Legwarmers (all sizes)
With 4mm (No.8) needles and A cast on 50 sts and cont in K1, P1 rib. Work 8 rows.
Inc 1 st at beg and end of next and every following 8th row until there are 88 sts on the needle.
Cont without shaping until 168 rows have been worked from cast on.
Cast off in rib.
To make up
Press work according to instructions on ball band. Join left shoulder seam and collar of dress. Sew in sleeves. Join side and sleeve seams. Join leg seam of legwarmers. Press seams.

Variations
a) Make the dress shorter for a stunning mini-dress, or shorter still, for a sweater.
b) Combine two or three different yarns to obtain the same thickness as the original pattern. How about mohair plus lurex plus bouclé – for a really unusual effect!

94

24 Tracksuit

MADE IN A SILKY FABRIC FOR EVENINGS

MADE IN COTTON JERSEY WITH APPLIQUÉ INITIAL AND SLEEVE STRIPES

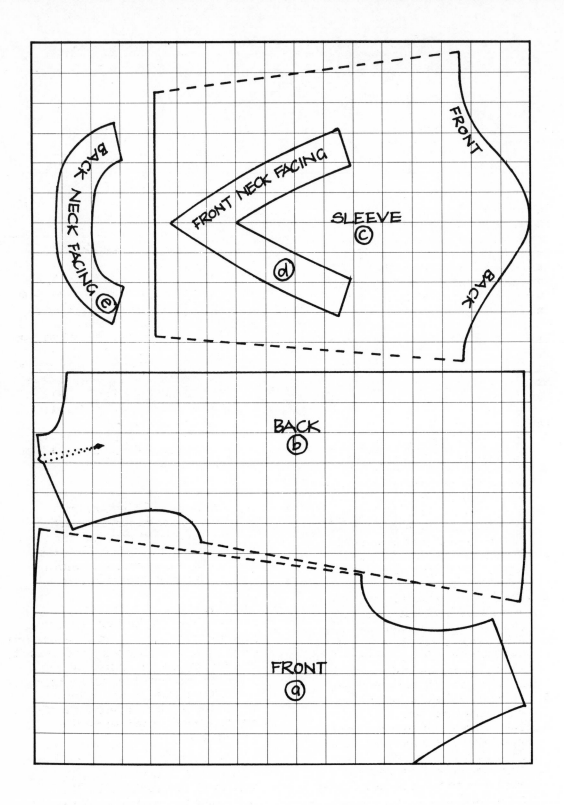

BACK NECK FACING (e)

FRONT NECK FACING (d)

SLEEVE (c)

FRONT

BACK

BACK (b)

FRONT (a)

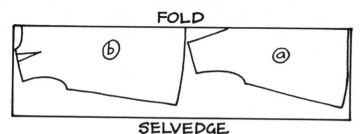

FOLD

SELVEDGE

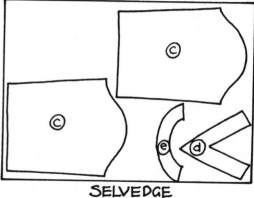

SELVEDGE

SELVEDGE

No, we don't expect you to go jogging round the block just at this moment – but how about those relaxation classes, or gardening, or simply for around the house? Tracksuits are really wonderfully practical and comfy, and the top can be worn with other things too.

Fabric: *Top:* 2.90m ($3\frac{1}{4}$yd) of 90cm (36in) wide fabric. *Trousers:* 2.40m ($2\frac{5}{8}$yd) of 90cm (36in) wide fabric.
Notions: 3.50m (4yd) of 2.5cm (1in) wide elastic.

Top

1. Take the back section, mark and sew the two back neck darts. Press.
2. Take front and back sections and with right sides together, pin and sew shoulder seams. Press seams open.
3. Take front and back neck facings, and with right sides together sew both shoulder seams. Press seams open. Neaten outside edge of facing with zig-zag stitching or oversewing (see 'How To' Guide).
4. With right sides together and taking care to match shoulder seams, pin and sew facing to neckline of top. Trim seam and clip, turn through to inside of tracksuit top and press. Top-stitch all round neck edge, a machine foot space away from the neck edge.
5. With right sides together, sew both side seams. Press seams.
6. Take sleeve section and with right sides together sew underarm seam. Press. Repeat with second sleeve.
7. Turn over and stitch a 6mm ($\frac{1}{4}$in) hem all round sleeve bottom. Repeat on second sleeve.

8. Then turn up a further 4cm ($1\frac{1}{2}$in) around the bottom of both sleeves and stitch, leaving a small gap through which to insert the elastic.
9. Pin in and sew both sleeves (see 'How To' Guide).
10. Turn up and sew a 6mm ($\frac{1}{4}$in) hem all round bottom edge of tracksuit top and then a further 4cm ($1\frac{1}{2}$in) hem. Sew, leaving a small gap through which to insert elastic.
11. Slot elastic through hem, draw up to fit and secure. Repeat this with both sleeve hems.

Trousers

12. Cut pattern 17 and make up according to the instructions, but omit shirring at waist and turn over a 6mm ($\frac{1}{4}$in) hem followed by a 4cm ($1\frac{1}{2}$in) hem stitched down with a small gap left to insert elastic.

Variations

a) Make the basic tracksuit, but with a slight difference – make it in soft and supple cotton jersey for more comfort and less bulk.
b) Appliqué contrast stripes and a huge American-style initial on your top before you make it up (see 'How To' Guide).
c) For a really different evening outfit make the tracksuit up in something sleek and slippery.

N.B. With that odd piece of fabric left over, why not make yourself a natty little bag for your tracksuit? Just use the instructions for the wash bag, pattern 32.

97

25 Sunsuit

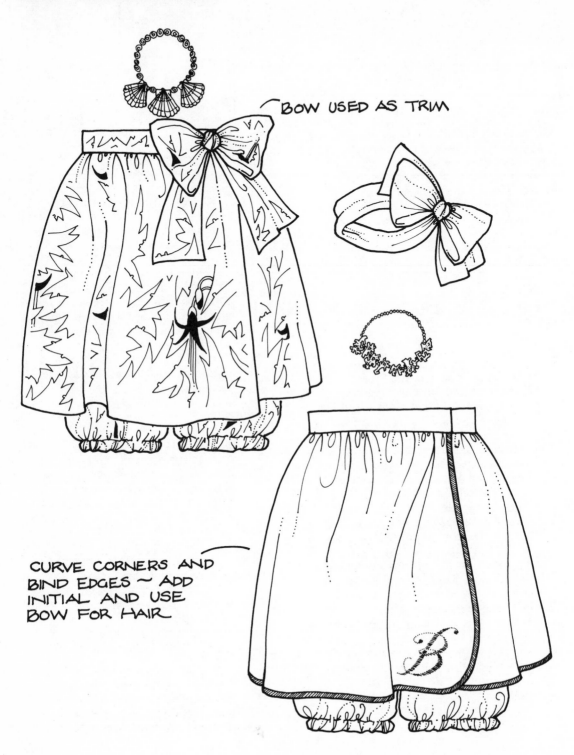

BOW USED AS TRIM

CURVE CORNERS AND
BIND EDGES ~ ADD
INITIAL AND USE
BOW FOR HAIR

98

Zany sunsuit, and yet it serves a really useful purpose. It covers up all those places which need covering and lets you expose the rest of you to those glorious healthful rays. Make it bold and bright or plain and sophisticated.

Sizes: One size fits sizes 10 to 14.
Fabric: 2.30m ($2\frac{1}{2}$yd) of 115cm (45in) wide fabric.
Notions: Hook and eye; press stud; 2.00m ($2\frac{1}{4}$yd) of 6mm ($\frac{1}{4}$in) wide elastic.

Top

1. With right sides together, place one band on the other and sew round two short and one long edge.
2. Clip corners and trim seams, turn out and press.
3. With right sides together, sew the three body sections together along their longest sides, thus forming one large strip.
4. Turn over and sew a 6mm ($\frac{1}{4}$in) turning along the two short edges, then a further hem of 2cm ($\frac{3}{4}$in) and stitch down.
5. Run a line of gathering along one long edge and draw up until it is the same length as the band.
6. With right sides together pin gathered edge of body section to one raw edge (single thickness) of underarm band. Space gathers out evenly and then stitch down. Trim seam.
7. Turn under the seam allowance on the remaining raw edge of band and slipstitch it down to previous line of stitching. Press.
8. Try on the sunsuit, wrapping the right side over the left. Sew on hook and eye at the edge of the top wrap-over. Then sew a press stud at the edge of the band underneath to secure.
9. Turn up hem as desired.
10. Take two bow sections and with right sides together, sew them together to form one long strip. Repeat with second two bow sections. Press seams open.
11. Take these two long bow sections and with right sides together, sew them together down two long and one short

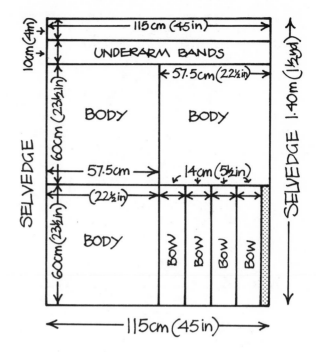

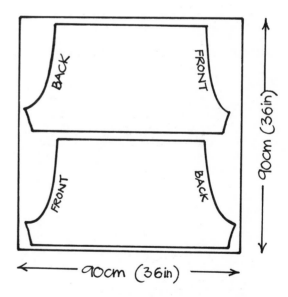

side. Trim seams, clip corners, turn out and press. Slipstitch short end closed.
12. Stitch bow section to band 2.5cm (1in) in from the edge of the top wrap, by slipstitching through the centre seam of the bow section, ruching it slightly to fit. Tie bow neatly.

99

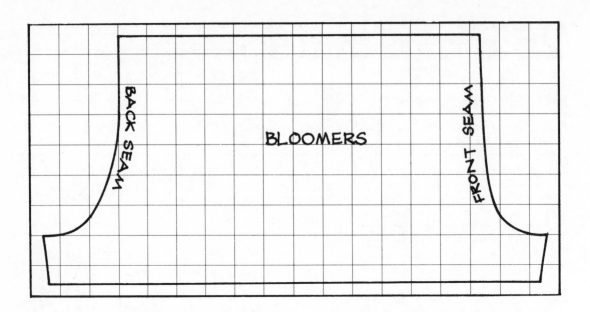

BACK SEAM

BLOOMERS

FRONT SEAM

Bloomers

13. Take two bloomer sections and, with right sides together, sew centre front then centre back seams. Trim, clip and neaten seams.

14. Then with right sides together sew crutch seam. Trim, neaten and press seam.

15. Turn over and stitch a 6mm ($\frac{1}{4}$in) turning all round top edge of bloomers and around both leg openings.

16. Turn over a further 13mm ($\frac{1}{2}$in) hem around top edge and leg openings, leaving a small opening through which to insert elastic.

17. Insert elastic through waist channel and draw up to fit. Do not cut the

ends of the elastic off, but tie a knot and leave a few inches extra hanging on the inside of the bloomers. Then as your waistline grows you can let out a little elastic to retain a good fit.

18. Insert elastic into bloomer legs, draw up to fit, cut off and secure.

Variations

a) Really go over the top with a big, bold tropical print and lots of colours to add zing to summer.

b) As a total contrast use a fine, plain-coloured cotton jersey. Curve the edges of the hem and bind it with contrast binding. Then add a luscious, heavily embroidered monogram. Use the bow to tie up your hair!

100

26 Wraps and scarves

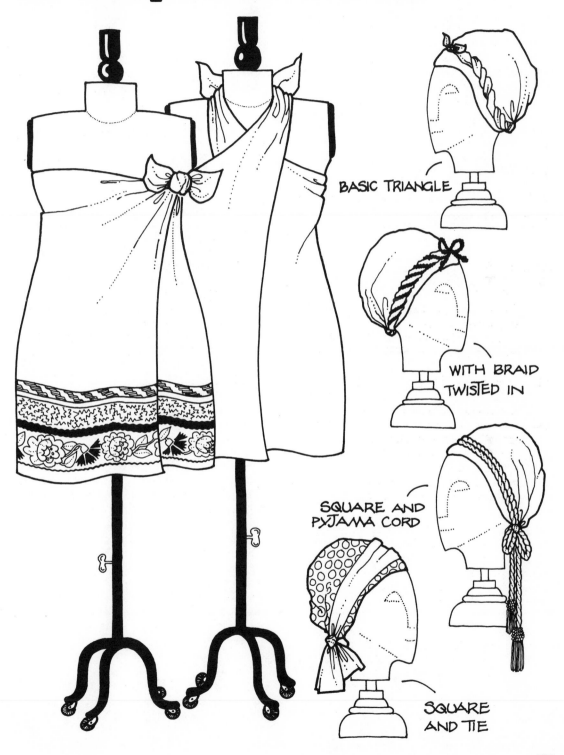

BASIC TRIANGLE

WITH BRAID TWISTED IN

SQUARE AND PYJAMA CORD

SQUARE AND TIE

101

Kangas are an ideal form of clothing for holidays, or just plain hot weather. One piece of fabric simply tied around the body – what could be better on a scorching hot day? No restrictions at all – perfect.

And, on days when your hair is looking a little less than its glamorous best, try out some of these natty ways with headscarves. Make them to mix and match with day or evening wear.

The permutations are too numerous to mention. Simply let your imagination run riot, mixing and matching the most glorious fabrics to tone or contrast with your clothes.

Sizes: For all these patterns one size fits sizes 10 to 14.

Tie scarf
Fabric: 15cm x 1.50m (6in x $1\frac{5}{8}$yd) piece of fabric with raw edges hemmed.

Fold in half lengthways, sew the long edge and one short edge. Trim seams, turn out and press. Slipstitch the short open end together.

Kanga
Fabric: 1.75m x 1.10m (2yd x $1\frac{1}{4}$yd) piece of fabric with raw edges hemmed.
The basic tie
The simplest way to wear the Kanga is to wrap it around you high up under your arms, bath towel style, and tie it at one side. Or you can wear it as a skirt, tied around your waist – then wear the tie scarf as a bikini top tied at the back.
Cross-over method
To make a more interesting dress, wrap the Kanga around your back, bring it round high up under your arms, and then grasp one top corner in each hand, holding your arms straight out in front of you. Then cross one side over the other, swopping corners. Pull the ends up and tie them halter-style behind your neck.

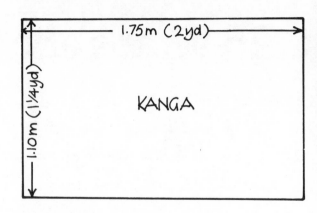

Variations
a)   Use brightly coloured floral or geometric prints for maximum effect.
b)   Why not tie-dye a piece of plain fabric for a really authentic looking Kanga?
c)   For an even bolder, more individual look paint huge tropical birds and flowers onto the Kanga with fabric paint.

Triangle scarf
Fabric: Triangular piece of fabric, hemmed all round, 1.50m ($1\frac{5}{8}$yd) along longest side and 50cm (20in) at deepest point.

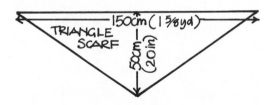

Find the centre of the long straight edge and position it low on your brow, between the eyebrows (with triangle point hanging down at the back of your head). Next take the two long ends and tie them over the triangle at the back of your neck. Now twist these two long strings round and round to form two twisted cords, bring them round to the front of your head and tie with a double knot. Twist the two tiny ends back into the twisted band. Tuck in the tiny triangle at the back.

Variation
After having tied the knot at the back of the neck, take 1.00m (1yd) of braid or cord and find the centre point. Match the centre

102

point of the braid to the knot, then take up the braid and the scarf ends and twist them together. Now knot at the front in the usual way.

Square scarf

Fabric: 70 x 70cm (28 x 28in) square of fabric, hemmed all round.

The evening tie

Take the square and fold over to form a double triangle, tie around the head in the same way as the triangular scarf. But this time tuck in the short ends and fold up the triangle flap and tuck that in too. Take a silky tasselled dressing gown cord, wrap it around your head twice and tie at the back, letting the tassels drape over your shoulder.

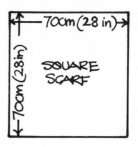

The day tie

Tie the square scarf as before, but this time wrap a long tie scarf (see above) around it and knot at the back. Let the ends hang free.

LINGERIE

27 Flouncy waist slip

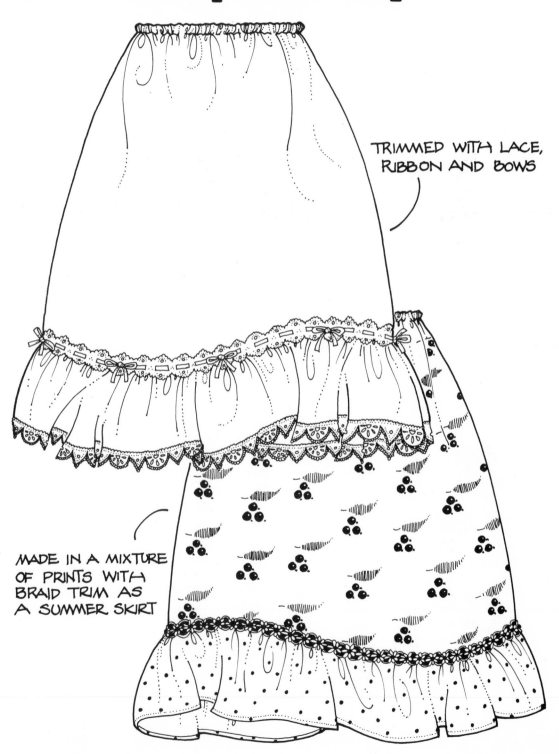

TRIMMED WITH LACE, RIBBON AND BOWS

MADE IN A MIXTURE OF PRINTS WITH BRAID TRIM AS A SUMMER SKIRT

Maternity dresses and skirts have lots more fabric in them than normal styles, so you'll need a pretty waistslip to give your dresses a better line. This one is easy to make and can be made as plain or as fancy as you like.

Sizes: One size fits sizes 10 to 14.
Fabric: 1.60m ($1\frac{3}{4}$yd) of 90cm (36in) wide fabric.
Notions: 2.70m (3yd) of broderie anglaise or lace trim; narrow elastic.

1. Take front and back sections and, with right sides together, sew side seams using a felled seam (see 'How To' Guide).
2. Turn over and stitch down a tiny hem around top edge. Then turn down a 2cm ($\frac{3}{4}$in) hem all round top edge. Stitch down leaving a small gap at centre back to insert elastic.
3. Take the three frilled sections, and with right sides together join all short ends to form a circle. Press and neaten seams.
4. Run a line of gathering around top edge of frill and draw up gently.
5. With right sides together pin to hem of slip, arrange gathers evenly, tack and sew seam. Neaten seam edge.
6. Run narrow elastic through the channel, try on slip and adjust elastic to fit. Do not cut elastic but simply knot it and leave the ends tucked inside the slip. Then as you grow you can let out the elastic.
7. Turn up and stitch hem as desired. Stitch on broderie anglaise or lace.

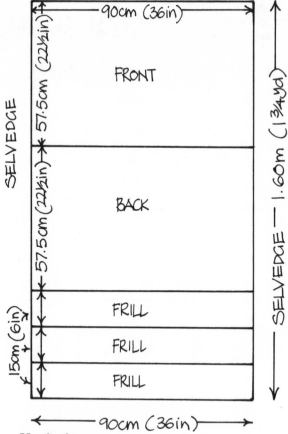

Variations
a) Trim this simple slip with as much gorgeous lace and ribbons as you like, perhaps letting it show just a little below your dress.
b) For a summer skirt you can make it in a flower print or a check, trimmed with braid. Or, if you're feeling really brave, a huge Hawaiian print.

106

28 Softly gathered nightdress

MADE AS A SUN DRESS WITH FABRIC OR RIBBON TIES THREADED WITH BEADS AND ENDS KNOTTED

MADE IN VIYELLA WITH PLAIN STRAPS AND WORN OVER A BLOUSE

MADE AS A NIGHTIE IN FINE LAWN WITH SHIRRED STRAPS

This really pretty nightie is so simple to make, even the absolute beginner should find it easy. Start with the basic nightie and this will give you the confidence to attempt one of the pretty dress versions and then progress to something a bit more ambitious.

Softly gathered nightdress
Sizes: One size fits sizes 10 to 14
Fabric: 2m ($2\frac{1}{4}$yd) of 90cm (36in) wide cotton/polyester fabric.
Notions: Shirring elastic.

1. With right sides together, match front and back pieces and sew side seams

using a felled seam. (See 'How To' Guide.)
2. Turn over a tiny double hem at top edge and stitch.
3. Starting 2cm ($\frac{3}{4}$in) down from top edge, machine 9 rows of shirring all round top of dress. (See 'How To' Guide.)
4. Take one strap section and sew a tiny double hem all round. Repeat with second strap.
5. Machine four rows of shirring down centre of each strap.
6. Try on dress. Pin straps in place, stretching slightly. Slipstitch to inside of nightdress along shirring lines.
7. Turn up desired hem.

Brushed cotton pinafore
Sizes: One size fits sizes 10 to 14.
Fabric: 2m ($2\frac{1}{4}$yd) of 90cm (36in) wide fabric.
Notions: Shirring elastic.

1. Repeat steps 1-3 of basic nightdress instructions.
2. Take one front and one back strap sections and with right sides together sew round one short and two long sides. Turn through and press, slipstitch short end closed. Press and topstitch all round. Repeat with second strap.
3. Try on dress and pin then slipstitch the straps to the inside, along the lines of shirring.
4. Turn up hem as desired.

N.B. The straps of this dress don't actually support it – the shirring does. Therefore they don't need to be attached too securely, but always pin the straps in place with the shirring slightly stretched.

Frilled sundress
Sizes: One size fits sizes 10 to 14.
Fabric: 2.20m ($2\frac{1}{2}$yd) of 90cm (36in) wide cotton fabric.
Notions: Shirring elastic; optional ribbon and beads.

1. Repeat steps 1 to 3 of nightdress instructions.
2. Take the three frill sections, and with right sides together sew short ends

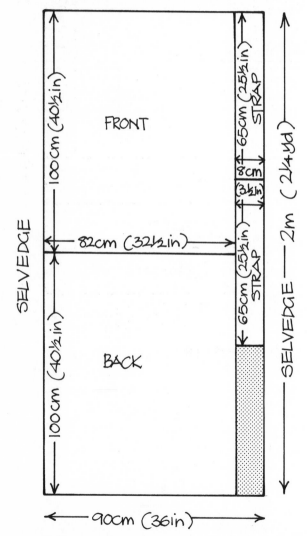

Softly gathered nightdress

108

together to form a circle.

3. Run a gathering line around one edge and draw up.

4. With right sides together pin to hem of dress, spacing out gathers evenly. Stitch seam, then neaten.

5. Make flat ties, 50cm (20in) long, from the excess fabric (see 'How To' Guide). Or use narrow satin ribbons trimmed with beads.

6. Try on dress and pin straps into place on the inside of the dress. Slipstitch into place. Tie in bows on shoulders.

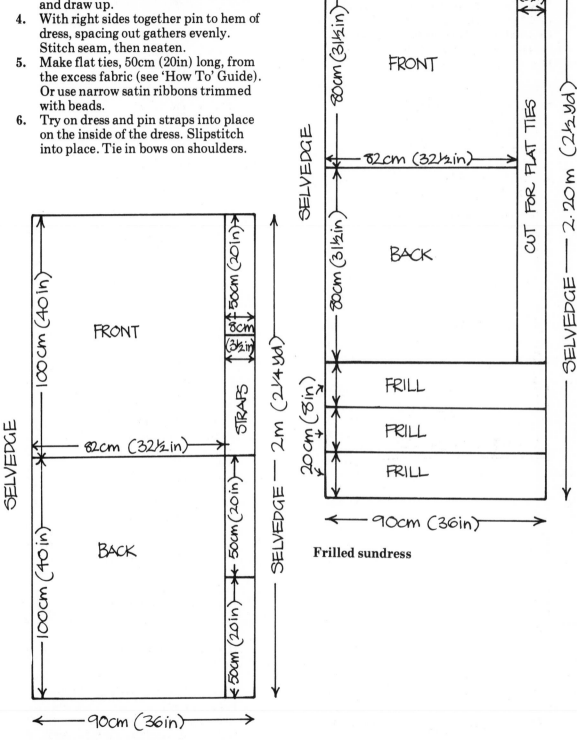

Frilled sundress

Brushed cotton pinafore

29 Lacy knit bedjacket

MADE IN MOHAIR WITH CROCHET EDGING

SATIN BINDING

MOHAIR/LUREX MIXTURE

EDGED WITH LACE AND RIBBON THREADED THROUGH HOLES

110

Bedjackets most definitely are not restricted to maiden aunts and grannies. This delicate, lacy-look jacket is marvellous for hospital wear and useful too for slipping on when it's time for junior's night-time feed.

Yarn: Of Mohair: 5/5 x 50g balls.
Needles: A pair of 5mm (No.6) and a 4.5mm crochet hook.
Tension: 14 sts and 24 rows to 10cm (4in) square, measured over pattern on 5mm (No.6) needles.
Measurements: To fit sizes 10 to 12/12 to 14. *Length:* 47/50cm (18½/19½in). *Sleeve seam:* 23/23cm (9/9in).

Back
With 5mm (No.6) needles cast on 65/73 sts and cont in patt thus:
Row 1: K1, (yrn to M1, K3, M1, K1).
Row 2: P.
Row 3: K1, (K1, sl 1, K2 tog, PSSO, K2).
Row 4: P.
These 4 rows form the pattern.
Cont until 58/64 rows have been worked from cast on.
Shape armholes: Keeping patt correct cast off 4/6 sts at beg of next 2 rows (57/61 sts). Dec 1 st at beg of next and every following row until 47/49 sts rem.
Cont without shaping until 112/118 rows have been worked from cast on.
Shape shoulders: Keeping patt correct cast off 12/13 sts at beg of next 2 rows.
Cast off rem 23 sts.

Right front
With 5mm (No.6) needles cast on 33/37 sts and cont in patt as given for back until 59/65 rows have been worked from cast on.
Shape armhole: Next row: Keeping patt correct cast off 4/6 sts, patt to end.
Next row: Patt to end.
Dec 1 st at beg of next and every following alt row until 24/25 sts rem.
Cont without shaping until 90/96 rows have been worked from cast on.
Shape neck: Next row: Keeping patt correct cast off 7 sts, patt to end.
Next row: Patt to end.
Dec 1 st at beg of next and every following alt row until 12/13 sts rem.
Cont without shaping until 113/119 rows

have been worked from cast on.
Cast off.
Left front
With 5mm (No.6) needles cast on 33/37 sts and cont in patt as given for back until 58/64 rows have been worked from cast on.
Shape armhole: Next row: Keeping patt correct cast off 4/6 sts, patt to end.
Next row: Patt to end.
Dec 1 st at beg of next and every following alt row until 24/25 sts rem.
Cont without shaping until 89/95 rows have been worked from cast on.
Shape neck: Next row: Keeping patt correct cast off 7 sts, patt to end.
Next row: Patt to end.
Dec 1 st at beg of next and every following alt row until 12/13 sts rem.
Cont without shaping until 112/118 rows have been worked from cast on.
Cast off.
Sleeves (2 alike)
With 5mm (No.6) needles cast on 49/53 sts and cont in patt as given for back.
Work 54/54 rows.
Shape sleeve head: Keeping patt correct cast off 4/6 sts at beg of next 2 rows.
Dec 1 st at beg and end of next and every following 4th row until 19 sts rem.
Cast off.
To make up
Do not press. Join shoulder seams. Sew in sleeves, gathering sleeve heads in to fit armholes. Sew side and sleeve seams.
Make crochet edging thus:
Work 1 row of double crochet along edge of knitting.
Row 2: 3ch, 3tr into first tr, * miss 3tr, 1dc into next tr, 3ch, 3tr into same tr, repeat from * to end, working extra clusters when turning corners and ending with: miss 3tr, 1dc into t.ch. Fasten off.

Variations
a)   If crochet isn't one of your strong points, then edge the jacket with lace trimming.
b)   Knit it in lurex and mohair mix to make a stunning evening jacket.
c)   For an even more feminine look, slot ribbon round the neck and cuffs. Draw up into gathers and tie in bows.

30 Kimono robe

MADE IN A MIXTURE OF ORIENTAL COTTON PRINTS

MADE IN SPRIGGED AND PLAIN COTTON WITH LACE TRIM

112

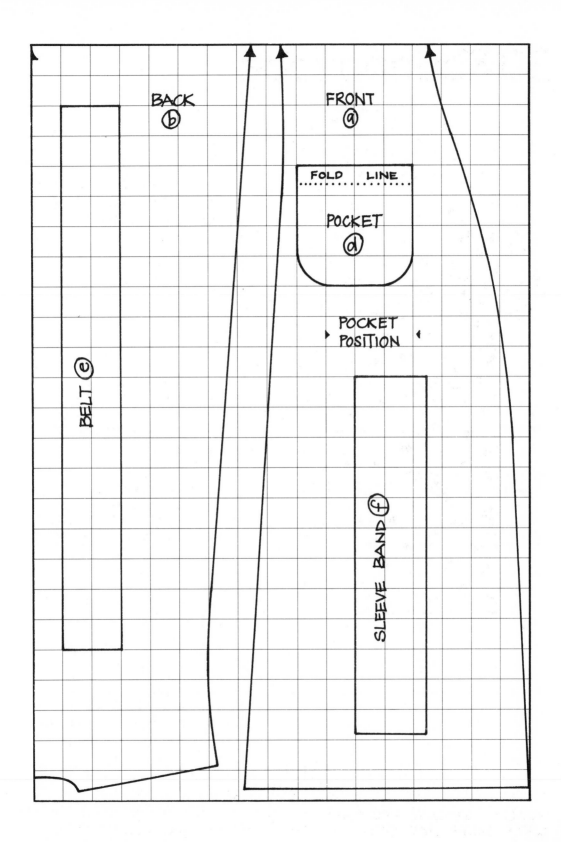

BACK ⓑ

FRONT ⓐ

FOLD   LINE

POCKET ⓓ

POCKET POSITION

BELT ⓔ

SLEEVE BAND ⓕ

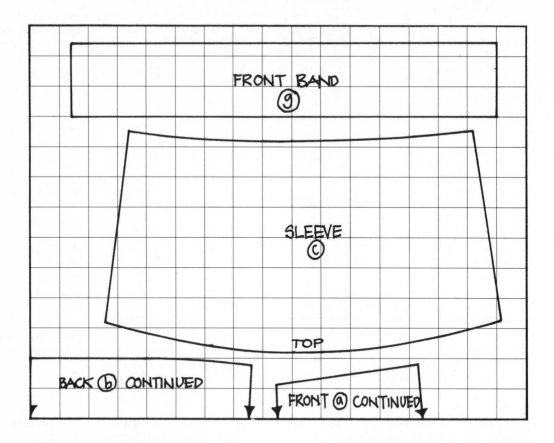

FRONT BAND
ⓖ

SLEEVE
ⓒ

TOP

BACK ⓑ CONTINUED

FRONT ⓐ CONTINUED

Wrap-around kimono robe, very basic but still the best style for an easy to make and comfortable garment. Trim it just as you like with lace or embroidery. Remember not to make it too long – you might just trip over the hem whilst carrying the baby.

Sizes: One size fits sizes 10 to 14.
Fabric: 2.80m ($3\frac{1}{8}$yd) of 140cm (54in) fabric.

1. Take pocket section and, with right sides together, fold over flap and stitch a 1.5cm ($\frac{5}{8}$in) seam at each side of flap. Clip corners, turn out and press. Press a 1.5cm ($\frac{5}{8}$in) hem all round rest of pocket. Pin and topstitch pocket in place. Repeat with second pocket.
2. Take two back sections and with right sides together, match to front sections and sew shoulder seams. Press and fell. (See 'How To' Guide.)

3. Open out dressing gown flat with right side uppermost. With right sides together, match centre of sleeve top with shoulder seam and sew sleeve in flat. Repeat with second sleeve. Press and fell seams.
4. With right sides together, and taking care to match armhole seams, sew underarm and side seam in one. Neaten this seam. Repeat with second side seam.
5. Take the two front band sections and with right sides together, sew together at one short edge. Press open. Fold over and press a 1.5cm ($\frac{5}{8}$in) hem along one long edge.
6. With right sides together and matching centre back seam of band to centre back seam of dressing gown, pin and sew the long, unfolded edge of band up left front, across neck and down right side. Press seam allowance towards band.
7. Neaten, then turn up and sew a 2.5cm

114

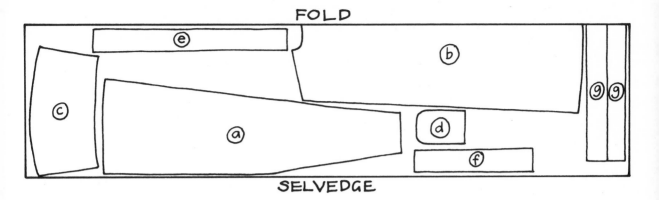

FOLD

SELVEDGE

(1in) hem all round kimono hem. Do not sew across bottom of front bands – simply press them up.

8. Fold front band in half to inside, turning it back as far as previous sewing line. Tack, press and topstitch band down. Press fold edge and remove tacking.

9. Take two belt sections and with right sides together, sew short ends together. Press open. Fold belt in half lengthways, with right sides together. Sew all round raw edges, leaving a small gap in the centre of one long edge. Trim seam allowance, turn out and press. Slipstitch the opening.

10. Take sleeve band and with right sides together, sew across short ends to form a circle. Press seam open. Press

up a 1.5cm ($\frac{5}{8}$in) hem all round one edge. Stitch the remaining raw edge to sleeve hem (with right sides together and matching underarm seams). Press seam allowance towards the band.

11. Fold band to inside, matching edge to previous stitching line. Topstitch down.

Variations

a) Make the kimono robe in a lightweight, brightly coloured cotton print – ideal for hospital wear.

b) Pretty it up by tucking flounced trim with a broderie anglaise frill under the front bands and sleeve bands.

c) Shorten the pattern and make it up in towelling for a super beach robe.

115

31 Holdall and matching slippers

BAG MADE IN QUILTED FABRIC WITH WEBBING STRAPS

SLIPPERS MADE IN LINEN WITH CROSS STITCH EMBROIDERED TOPS

SLIPPERS MADE IN SPRIGGED COTTON WITH PATCHWORK BLOCK TOPS

Roomy, quilted bag to hold all those vital things you'll have packed weeks before the final dash to the hospital. Useful too as a weekend bag later. To match, there are some snug mule slippers. Why not make these to match your bedjacket and dressing gown too?

Holdall
Fabric: 90cm (1yd) of 90cm (36in) wide quilted fabric.
Notions: Bias binding; 2m (2¼yd) of 5cm (2in) wide webbing; 46cm (18in) zipper.

1. To make strap, lay webbing evenly onto bag sections and pin into place (see diagram). Topstitch up each side of the webbing, then stitch a cross shape 10cm (4in) away from top edge.
2. Bind both top zip edges with bias binding (see 'How To' Guide).
3. Tack and sew in zipper.
4. With right sides together sew base seam and press.
5. Pin and sew in gussets.
6. Turn out bag.
7. For a firmer base to the bag, cut out a piece of cardboard to fit and slip it inside.

Slippers
Sizes: To fit all sizes.
Fabric: 50cm (¾yd) of 90cm (36in) wide quilted fabric.
Notions: Bias binding.

Making the pattern
Making a personally sized slipper pattern is very easy to do and once you've made one pair you can go on to make them for the whole family.

1. Sit in a firm chair and place a piece of paper on the floor in front of you.
2. Put your foot on the paper, spreading your toes slightly. Take a pencil and draw round the outline, taking care not to let the pencil slope under your foot.
3. Place this paper onto a firm surface and re-draw the outline to even up the wobbly shape. Then add 1.5cm (⅝in) all round to allow for a seam turning.

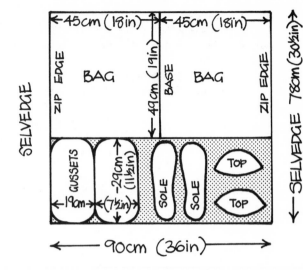

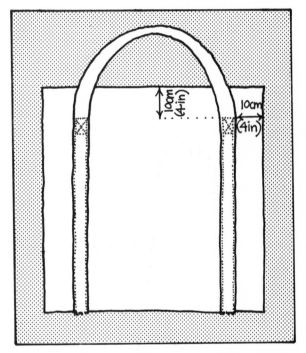

Cut out this shape to form pattern for sole.
4. Now mark a point 14cm (5½in) down from the topmost point of the foot shape, and rule a line right across the pattern.
5. Trace off this top half of the shape onto pattern paper and cut out.
6. Place your foot flat on the floor once again and measure over the instep

117

down to the floor on both sides. Then add 3cm ($1\frac{1}{2}$in).

7. Take the pattern piece you have already made for the top half of the slipper and make several cuts with the scissors from the straight base up towards the toe (cut practically to the top but not right through). Then fan the pattern piece out until the base measures the same as your instep plus 3cm ($1\frac{1}{2}$in) (see point 6 above).

8. Draw round this new shape, making the base line straight again. You now have your slipper pattern.

Making the slippers

9. Cut out the slipper sections remembering to reverse the pattern pieces to fit the second foot.

10. Bind across the straight edge of the slipper top section. (See 'How To' Guide.)

11. With right sides uppermost on both pieces pin the slipper top to the sole and tack.

12. Bind all round with bias binding, starting and ending at centre back of sole.

13. Repeat with second slipper.
NB. For a non-slip sole, you could buy a pair of large-size men's insoles, trim them to size and glue to the soles of the slippers.

Variations

a) Make the bag and slippers in corduroy with woven carpet braid trim.

b) If you like canvas-work embroidery then why not decorate the slipper tops with your own designs.

c) Decorate the bag and slippers with brightly coloured appliqué or patchwork.

d) Make the shoulder straps (just use longer lengths of braid or webbing) from brightly coloured, woven Peruvian belts.

32 Shower hat, wash bag and make-up purse

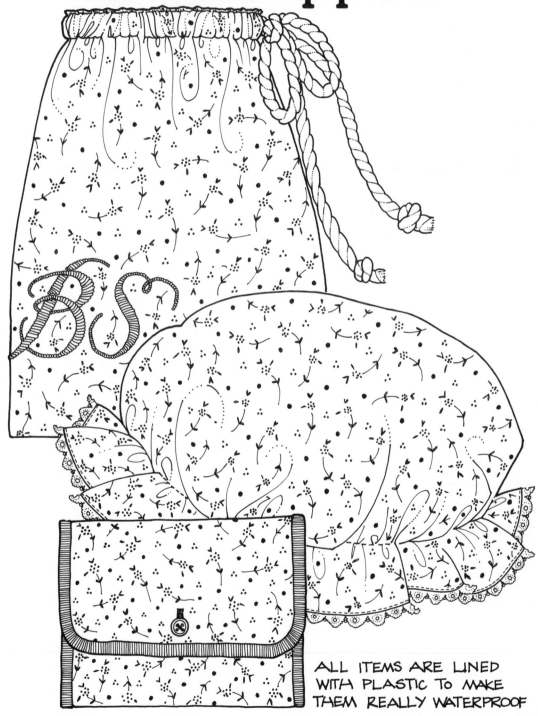

ALL ITEMS ARE LINED
WITH PLASTIC TO MAKE
THEM REALLY WATERPROOF

More handy accessories to slip into your hold all. They're all plastic-lined to cope with spills and splashes, and they wash easily too. Marvellous next year too, to take on holiday!

Hat

Sizes: One size fits all sizes.
Fabric: 50cm ($\frac{3}{4}$yd) of 115cm (45in) wide fabric; the same amount of thin shower curtain plastic.
Notions: Narrow elastic; 2m ($2\frac{1}{4}$yd) of narrow lace.

1. Cut out the circle once in fabric and once in plastic. Trim away 1.5cm ($\frac{5}{8}$in) all round the plastic circle.
2. With wrong sides together place plastic circle on top of fabric circle, leaving an excess of fabric all round. Turn this over the plastic and stitch down all round.
3. Pin lace all round underside of hat and slipstitch down.
4. Take some narrow elastic and cut off a length which fits comfortably around your forehead.
5. Stitch elastic all round the circle (on the inside) 2.5cm (1in) away from the fabric edge, stretching it slightly as you sew. Fasten off securely.

Wash bag

Fabric: 50cm ($\frac{3}{4}$yd) of 115cm (45in) wide fabric; the same amount of thin shower curtain fabric.
Notions: 1m ($1\frac{1}{8}$yd) of cord.

1. Cut out wash bag pattern in fabric and mark fold line. Do likewise with the plastic. With wrong sides together tack both pieces together close to the edges.
2. With fabric sides together fold along line, then machine across one short end and up the long side, stopping 10cm (4in) away from the top.
3. Turn back the seam allowance at the opening and stitch down. Turn the bag the right way out.
4. Turn over and stitch a tiny hem all round top. Then turn over and stitch a 2.5cm (1in) hem along the same edge. Stitch a second line very close to the top of the bag, forming a neat channel.

SELVEDGE

50cm (20in)
SHOWER HAT

35cm (14in)
WASH BAG
50cm (19½in)
115cm (45in)

13cm (5in)   13cm (5in)   9cm (3½in)
15cm (6in)   PURSE

←SELVEDGE 50cm (¾yd)→

5. Run the cord through the channel and knot. Knot the ends too.

Make-up purse

Fabric: Small strip of 115cm (45in) wide fabric; the same amount of thin shower curtain fabric.
Notions: Bias binding; press stud or button.

1. Cut out purse sections once in fabric and once in plastic.
2. Mark fold lines on fabric section.
3. With wrong sides together place fabric on top of plastic and tack all round.
4. With fabric sides together, fold front section up and tack seams up the sides of the purse.
5. Cut curves on flap corners.
6. Bind the outside edge of the purse, starting at one lower edge and finishing at the other. (See 'How To' Guide.)
7. Mark a position for fastening at centre front of flap, then attach a press stud or a button with a worked buttonhole.

Variations

a) Why not make these pretty accessories to match your kimono (pattern 30)?

b) Embroider them with lush satin monograms.

c) Use all those precious scraps to make them up in patchwork for something really unusual.

'How To' Guide

Neatening edges

When using fabrics that might possibly fray, it is worth spending a little time neatening the seam turnings by one of the following methods:

1. If you have a swing-needle sewing machine, zig-zag close to or slightly over the edge.

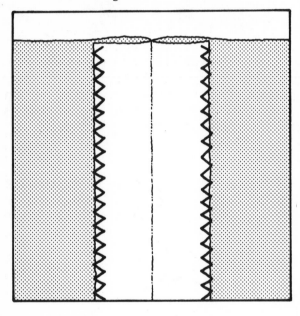

2. Oversew along raw edges by hand.

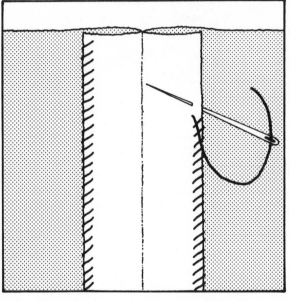

3. Use pinking shears when cutting out the pattern or when trimming seam allowances.

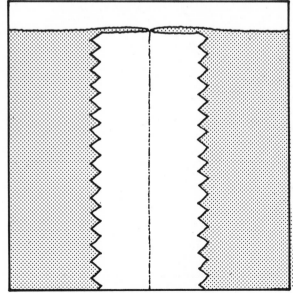

Felled seam

This is a very strong and useful seam which needs no neatening and is easier to sew than a French seam. It is ideal for fine fabrics. Sew the seam in the usual way but press both seam allowances to one side. Trim away the under seam allowance, turn the top seam allowance over it and press. Then topstitch down to conceal and enclose trimmed edge.

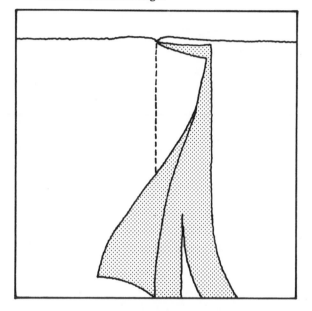

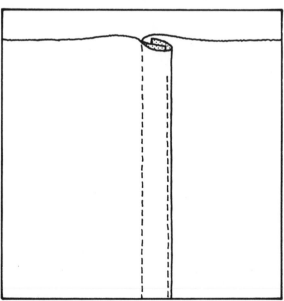

Pressing

To give any garment a professional finish, it is essential to press every seam as it is sewn. Use a large piece of muslin as a pressing cloth, dipped in water and wrung out as tightly as possible. Lay the garment on the ironing board, wrong side up. Press the seam open with your fingers, then lay the muslin over the seam and with the toe of the iron press the stitching of the seam lightly and quickly. Don't press the whole iron down flat and hard as this will leave ridges on the right side of your fabric. Allow the fabric to cool slightly before you move it from the board.

Clipping curves

When a seam is curved, trim away excess seam allowance after sewing and clip with scissors – towards but not too close to the stitching line. Then press.

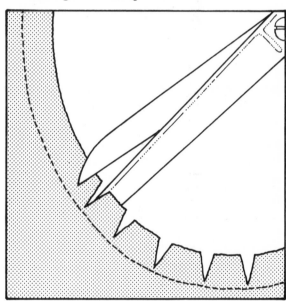

123

Topstitching

One thing that prevents your clothes from looking 'home made' is lots of decorative topstitching. It needs to be carefully done without kinks or wobbles. For instance, when topstitching around a collar, start off by placing the outside edge of the machine foot against the outside edge of the collar. Keep the edge of the foot running along the edge of the collar as you stitch round. In this way, using the machine foot as a guide, you can keep your topstitching parallel with either edges or seams (as for jeans).

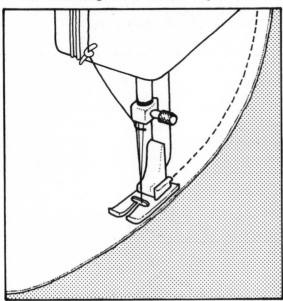

Binding

This is a neat way to finish off any kind of raw edge. The following instructions are for binding a neck or armhole, where the edges are curved. Straight edges are worked in the same way, but they're easier.

Take the bias binding and open out one edge. Place this edge, with right sides together, against the garment neck and pin – slightly stretching the binding as you go round the curves. Stitch down along fold, leaving 1.5cm ($\frac{5}{8}$in) of extra binding overlapping at centre back neck. Press this extra flap of binding under, to wrong side.

Fold the long free edge of the binding to inside neck so that the edge just covers the previous line of stitching. Tack down. With the right side uppermost, topstitch in the

dip between the bias and the fabric of the garment. (If you use closely matching thread, this stitching line will virtually disappear.) Slipstitch centre back join.

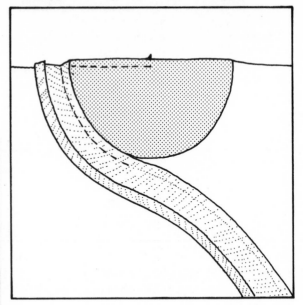

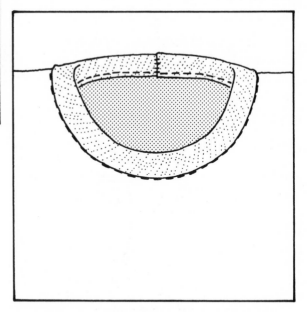

Stitching a curved hem

Stitch all round hem 6mm ($\frac{1}{4}$in) away from the edge. On the curved part of the hem, pull these stitches up slightly to take up excess fabric. Turn over a tiny hem along stitching line and then another hem the

124

required amount. Stitch down using herringbone or slipstitch. Press using a damp cloth – this will 'shrink' the gathering into place.

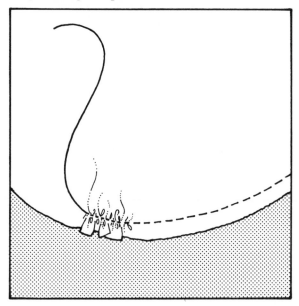

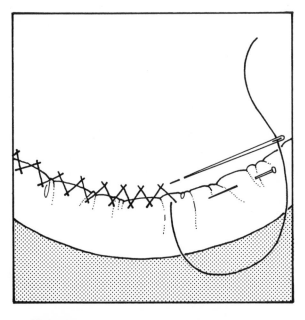

machine in the usual way and thread the top part of the machine with thread as normal. Set stitch length to the longest possible and, with the right side of the fabric uppermost, sew the lines of stitching a machine foot distance apart.

Appliqué
Sketch out the design lightly onto the background fabric. Trace off each individual shape, and cut out once in fabric and once in interfacing. Iron interfacing onto wrong side of shape, position on the fabric and tack down. Work a close zig-zag stitch round edge of shape. Pull out tacking.

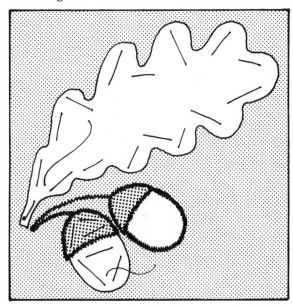

Shirring
Shirring is a very simple way of taking up excess fabric and making soft gathers, as well as giving garments shape and line. Take the shirring elastic and wind it onto the spool by hand. Put the spool into your

Setting in a sleeve

1. Sew underarm seam and press open.
2. Run a line of gathering stitches close to the edge of the fabric, around the crown of the sleeve. (Use the longest stitch length on machine.)
3. With right sides together match and pin the underarm seam of the sleeve to the side seam of the garment. Pin armhole on each side of seam up to gathering line.
4. Pin crown into armhole loosely (putting the pins at right angles to the edge.) Gather up the fullness very carefully and distribute any gathers evenly.
5. Tack along this seam line then sew into place. Trim and neaten.

Embroidery stitches

Here are two basic stitches to enable you to work a motif, such as the one on the yoke of the Western-style dress (pattern 2).

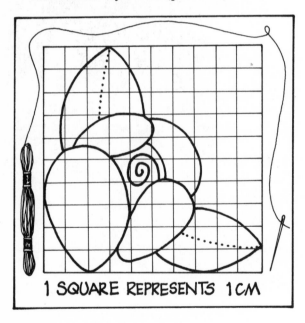

1 SQUARE REPRESENTS 1 CM

Chain stitch (for outlining)

Bring the thread out at the top of the line and hold it down with left thumb. Insert the needle back where it emerged and bring the point out a short distance further along the line inside the loop. Pull the thread through, keeping the working thread under the needle point. Repeat.

Satin stitch (for filling areas)

Use straight stitches worked closely together across the desired area. Try to keep a good edge, and don't make the stitches too long or the fabric will pucker. If the edge is uneven try outlining it with chain stitch.

Mattress stitch

This produces an invisible seam when sewing up knitted garments.

1. Place the pieces that are to be sewn together with edges parallel and right sides uppermost.
2. Use the same yarn as the garment (on garments made from fancy yarn such as bouclé, use a plain matching yarn), and work one stitch in from each edge. Pick up two rows at a time from each side and draw up.

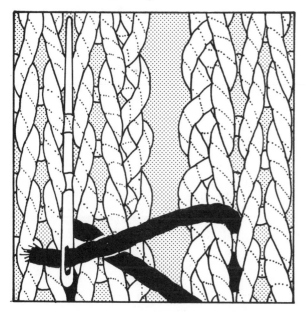

Flat ties

Take the tie section and fold both long outside edges to the centre, down whole length of strip. Press. Fold up short ends 6mm ($\frac{1}{4}$in) and press. Then fold down centre, matching outside edges together. Topstitch through, close to both edges.

Gathering

To achieve even and well balanced gathering, set your machine to its largest stitch length and sew two rows of machine stitching close to the edge that is to be gathered and well inside the seam allowance. Then take up the loose ends on the right side of the fabric and gently draw up. Space the gathers evenly and then tie the loose ends at each side of the work.

Swiss darning

An easy way to add decorative motifs to finished knitting.

1. Bring thread through to right side at base of stitch to be covered, then under the two threads of the stitch immediately above, from right to left.
2. Take thread back to wrong side through base of stitch. Continue in this manner until all the base line stitches have been worked.
3. Turn upside down and work second row in same manner, threading the needle through from right to left, under the threads of the stitch below.

Alternatives to buttonholes

If your sewing machine has no facility for making buttonholes, don't waste your time labouring over time-consuming hand embroidered versions. Here are a couple of quick alternatives.

1. Sew tiny plastic press studs (less bulk than metal press studs) in place of buttons and buttonholes. Then, on the outside of the garment, sew a 'false' button. This will give you the same look without the problems.
2. Use the new and very decorative snap studs. Put them on with a special hand operated tool for a secure finish.

127

Yarn

Brand names and manufacturers

No. 3	Ethnic winter dress	Pingouin Confortable
No. 5	Aran-style dress	Pingoland
No. 9	Chunky picture sweater	Pingoland
No. 10	Ribbed polo-neck sweater	Pingoland
No. 20	Bouclé jacket	Pingouin-Style Astrakan
No. 23	Balloon dress and legwarmers	Pingostar & Pingouin Meche Bouclee
No. 29	Lacy-knit bedjacket	Pingouin Laine et Mohair

For details of stockists write to:
French Wools Ltd.
7-11 Lexington Street
London W1R 4BU

Mail order available from:
Ries Wools
243 High Holborn
London WC2
Telephone: 01-242 7721

Acknowledgements

The authors acknowledge the help and advice they received from H.W. Peel and Company Limited who supplied the 'True Sew' pattern paper used for making up the patterns throughout this book. Details of local stockists can be obtained from the manufacturers H.W. Peel and Company Limited, Jeymer Drive, Greenford, Middx.

All the garments featured throughout this book were sewn with Gutermann 'Sew-all' 100% polyester thread, suitable for sewing all fabrics. Ribbon by Offray.

All shoes kindly loaned by Ivory Shoes.

Photographs by Chris Grout-Smith.

Photographic styling by Annie Oakes.

The following garments featured in the colour photographs were made up in Viyella (55% wool, 45% cotton) kindly supplied by the manufacturers:

Sailor smocks
Ethnic winter dress
Gathered trousers
Tailored overshirt
Gathered skirt
Pin-tucked blouse
Nightdress and kimono